I've been very grateful for the many group processes developed in the past decades that create new capacities and new relationships among people working together. Kate has brought the best of these together, in clear and direct language, making these processes easily accessible. Yet we must also notice how, in these past decades, we have become more separated, impatient and self-protective. Working well together is a much less frequent—even rare—experience as people withdraw in fear in response to profound uncertainty. This is where Kate's book becomes both a challenge and a gift. Can we commit to working in these ways so that people again become engaged with their work and manifest their collective creativity? If we do, people will remember the joy of what it feels like to work well together and produce work they believe in. And this is the ultimate gift.

MARGARET WHEATLEY, Author
Who Do We Choose To Be?

This book is a rare gem, as it's easily accessible, deeply useful and offers clear guidance to make changes that seem simple, but that will have profound effects, if practiced. Kate helps us to surface and make pragmatic what we intuitively know about groups and change processes. I urge you to see for yourself. It will strengthen your ability to navigate everything from relationships to complex systems, and to create the better outcomes we so need at this time.

NINA SIMONS
Co-Founder, Bioneers

At this time on our planet, learning to work together with open hearts and open minds is crucial to finding a just and sustainable path into the future. Kate has given us a wonderful guide for our journey forward together. *We Can Do This!* is a must-read for anyone working towards change in their communities, organizations or families.

LENA K. SOOTS
Faculty, Social Innovation at
Mount Royal University

Open any page of this book and you will find practical ideas and strategies for working with groups — as a facilitator, participant or manager. We will definitely use and share these tools!

Kate Sutherland has taken the leading theories of organizational development and done us the invaluable service of crystallizing, synthesizing, and connecting the very best models from the field. Most importanly, she makes them accessible and practical.

BRUCE SANQUIN, *The Advance Of Love*

Group work can be very demanding. The particular gift of *We Can Do This!* is one of companionship and encouragement. If you want to be refreshed, read this book. It will open you, remind you, and guide you to center in wellness and perform with greater mastery.

SYLVIA HOLLAND, Dialogue Associate
Morris J. Wosk Centre for Dialogue, Simon Fraser University

Kate's book is informative, relevant and very engaging. Many groups and organizations have difficulty describing their model of change or transformation. The ten frameworks that Kate has outlined allow all of us the opportunity to reflect upon our current approach, challenge our thinking, and create new possibilities personally and for our organizations. This book needs to be shared and discussed – allowing us to create new ways of learning and contributing to our communities.

JOHN TALBOT, Organizational Development Consultant

Often I am asked where the frontier in community engagement is. I believe that it's summarized in this beautiful book by Kate Sutherland, *We Can Do This!* It is the best summary of the processes that are leading community engagement and community development today, in my view.

DR. WENDY SARKISSIAN
Author and Community Engagement Specialist

Sutherland has assembled a tasting menu for anyone who has an appetite for sweet human interaction. Whether you are facilitating an interaction with yourself or with a group of a hundred or more, this is an invaluable book. Sutherland presents tools that are sophisticated and yet approachable. Using them moves the practice of facilitation from mechanical to magical!

ANNE KAYE, MANAGEMENT CONSULTANT AND CERTIFIED PROFESSIONAL FACILITATOR

Understanding group management theories as Kate lays out so simply and accessibly, is a huge benefit to anyone who relies on a group to get something done – whether it is a corporate team, a care circle that forms to take care of a sick friend, or a group of citizens who want to make their community stronger. I particularly love Kate's personalized, narrative voice that makes it seem like she wrote the book just for me. The book is information-packed, yet an easy read at the same time. I will definitely integrate many of the models and theories Kate explains so eloquently into the groups I work with.

ALISSA HAUSER, CO-FOUNDER, THE ENGAGE NETWORK

An easy read and essential guide for successful relating, founded in life-affirming values and truths. Sutherland has truly risen to the challenges of inner work and outer service, herein synthesizing years of experience with caring and insight.

MUKTI, MEDITATION TEACHER

My work has to do with transforming transportation into something that helps us live more equitably and more sustainably on the planet. This gets a lot more complicated as the world urbanizes, demographics shift, climate change makes its presence known, the economy restructures, and a responsive flurry of new technologies and services and systems arrive on the scene faster than we can figure out how they all fit together and what might be their effects. Suddenly transportation is as much about working together, connecting the dots, collaborating on multi-faceted solutions across disciplines and sectors as it is about engineering and infrastructure. I think Kate's book should be required reading at the very least for all transportation professionals if not for anyone who's responsible for making our cities and communities better.

SUSAN ZIELINSKI, FORMER MANAGING DIRECTOR SMART (SUSTAINABLE MOBILITY & ACCESSIBILITY RESEARCH & TRANSFORMATION) UNIVERSITY OF MICHIGAN

KATE SUTHERLAND

WE CAN DO THIS!

10 TOOLS TO UNLEASH OUR COLLECTIVE GENIUS

A guide for leaders, entrepreneurs, activists, managers, parents and anyone else who wants to work together better

INCITE
P R E S S
VANCOUVER, CANADA

Incite Press
Vancouver, British Columbia
Canada, V5V 5C8
incitepress@telus.net
www.WeCanDoThisTools.com

ORDERING INFORMATION

Quantity Sales. Discounts are available on quantity purchases. Contact Incite Press.

Individual Sales. Available through www.WeCanDoThisTools.com and online retailers, or by ordering into your local bookstore.

Editor: Saskia Wolsak. Copy Editors: Joanne Kembel and AAA WordSmith Documentation Services. Cover design: M80 Design Ltd – Wes Youssi. Illustrations: Michael Mann, Helen D'Sousa and Stina Brown. Text design: Tamara MacKenzie. Page Layout: Laura Redmond.

Printed in the United States of America. First Edition.

Cataloguing in Publication data is on file with Library and Archives Canada.

Sutherland, Kate, 1957-
We can do this! 10 tools to unleash our collective genius / by Kate Sutherland.
Includes bibliographical references.
ISBN 978-0-9866127-8-7

To Jill
Thank you for
being such a
visioneer &
Great love,
Kate

Dedicated to quickening peace and joy for you,
and everything you are connected to.

CONTENTS

Foreword

You have in your hands ten powerful tools – tools proven to make the world a better place for you, your family, friends, colleagues, society.

Tools that strengthen your ability to work together with others.

Tools that have been lovingly collected by a master practitioner.

Kate Sutherland knows what these tools are capable of. She has used them with skill, dexterity, and love for decades.

They are a practical response to a question so many of us have: "How can we work together better?"

In my own experience, one of the hardest parts of creating change has often been the frustrations of working with others, including colleagues. Despite my respect for them and appreciation of their values, too often competition, territoriality, and immaturity stand in the way.

The tools you now have access to are powerful because they reveal group dynamics previously hidden. They offer distilled wisdom for engaging with your colleagues, allies, and adversaries.

The tools are also powerful because they are about power – your personal power and the collective power of your constituency, membership, workforce, coalition, sector, or movement to work together beyond your wildest imaginings. They will help you find solutions for day-to-day challenges. They will also help create the popular receptivity and cultural support that will embolden even the most resistant of decision makers.

Kate Sutherland is part of a grand Canadian tradition that urges caution when handling powerful tools and technologies. These luminaries include economic historian Harold Innis and his disciple – the communications theorist Marshall McLuhan, the scientist and peace activist Ursula Franklin, and Canadian radio broadcaster Nora Young, the host of Spark – a program on the societal impact of new technologies. They understood as Kate clearly does how easy it is to mishandle any tool, to go astray, and yes, to abuse its purpose, if you are not grounded.

When I have been driven and single-minded in my pursuit of a cause, I have sometimes lost sight of how my actions affect others or how imbalances of power are playing out. Powerful tools can both heal and harm, so we need safety practices. It is so easy for us to recreate the same dynamics of injustice and dominance in our work for positive change, and this tendency must be lovingly resisted as Kate suggests in her pivotal chapter, "Groundwork."

This book would be a gift if it only offered clear, accessible descriptions of each tool and its practical purpose. Kate being Kate offers something more – an explanation of each tool's sacred potential. That, as you are about to discover, makes *We Can Do This!* a redemptive offering. This wise woman knows there can be no transformation without redemption.

The tools in *We Can Do This!* aren't miracle cures. But handling them with peaceful intent will work wonders in your life – and for your life's work.

So go ahead. Imagine. Create. And love the world you want into existence.

Al Etmanski
Surrey, Canada
August 2017

Preface

*"We can not solve our problems
with the same level of thinking that created them."*
—Albert Einstein

We are at a crossroads. What *has been* is breaking down all around us. Where we go from here depends on key choices, and especially our choice to believe that a life-sustaining civilization is possible.

As we feel our way forward – through the unknowns of creating new ways of being and doing in every aspect of society – we need collective intelligence, wisdom, and capacity as never before.

The intention of this book is to nourish and grow the capacity of emerging efforts for the bright future we sense is possible.

At the same time, this book is about you! Its deepest purpose is to support you to become the best *you* you can be, and then to help you keep on evolving, and in ways that ripple out through your life and everything you are connected with.

This collection of powerful tools is a vector of positive contagion for greater awareness. As the tools work *for* us, helping us navigate in our relationships, groups, and other human systems, they also work *on* us, shifting our perspectives, loosening the grip of our assumptions and judgments, and inviting us into the mystery of co-creating with Life.

The tools are profound and useful, *and* there is a deeper level in play: growing the consciousness of the ones (you and me) who are using the tools. The more each of us cultivates conscious awareness, the better we are able to foster positive change. As Bill O'Brien, puts it, "The success of an intervention depends on the interior condition of the intervener."[1]

I hope this excites you as much as it excites me. We can benefit from using the tools, and grow our consciousness at the same time.

Five years ago, when I released the first version of this book[2], I played down these deeper dimensions rather than risk alienating readers. Now I sense greater openness. There is a growing understanding that something very profound needs to shift if we are to find our way through the ecological, social, political, and spiritual crises of our time.

We live in a time of quickening – in the face of, and perhaps sometimes because of, so much that is darkening. It is time to activate the power of collective intention to shift consciousness individually and in our groups and other human systems.

There is a good chance you are already doing this work. I hope you will join me in growing the movement to revolutionize how we work in groups, while simultaneously helping us deepen the consciousness from which we operate.

Our children depend on it, as does all life on our beautiful planet.

---

1 Bill O'Brien is former CEO of Hanover Insurance. Source: Scharmer, Otto. *Theory U: Leading from the Future as It Emerges*. San Francisco, California: Berrett-Koehler Publishers, Inc., 2009, page 7.

2 Sutherland, Kate. *Make Light Work in Groups: 10 Tools to Transform Meetings, Companies and Communities*. Vancouver, Canada: Incite Press, 2012.

Introduction

*The real voyage of discovery consists not in seeking
new landscapes, but in having new eyes.*

Marcel Proust

We Can Do This! introduces ten tools to revolutionize how we work
together – in teams, organizations, companies, and communities.[1]

Most of us have had a taste of groups at their very best. Perhaps
it was a meeting where there was little ego and lots of heart, or a
conference that radically changed our way of thinking, or work
in a team that was in flow, on purpose, and getting things done.

Most of us have also experienced groups that are mildly to
extremely frustrating. Being in them is like being forced to eat
gruel. This is a tragedy. So much is lost and wasted in monotonous
or conflicted meetings, and in bureaucracies that seem structured
to stifle even the smallest wisp of inspiration and passion.

Perhaps even more is lost, however, in groups that are "good
enough." Things are not awful, the status quo is even comfortable,
but deep down our souls are suffocating for want of the oxygen
and aliveness that comes from expressing ourselves more fully.

The good news is that a few relatively simple shifts in perspective can help us transform group dynamics. Each group already has
everything it needs to change from humdrum or frustrating to

---

1   I will often use the word "groups" as shorthand for all human systems.

dynamic and fun. We just need to know where to look.

This book introduces my ten favourite tools for working in groups, organizations, and communities. These are the top ten ways of seeing and being that I have used to guide my consulting and facilitation work for the past twenty-five years.

I make no claim that these are the only tools, just that they are a versatile and powerful starter kit.

The ten tools

I think of these tools as theoretical and structural frameworks. A framework distills a small number of key variables and sets out what is important, what needs to change, and the main levers for making a difference.

A framework can also be like a lens in that it focuses our attention on specific aspects of a situation depending on its aperture, colour, and length.

Each of the ten tools is widely used by facilitators and organizational consultants, and each brings game-changing perspectives and insights. Taken together, they are like a toolbox with hammers, saws, screwdrivers, and "C" clamps – to support you no matter what the group's purpose and goals.

Much has been written about each of the frameworks – important books and articles and curricula. *We Can Do This!* is about making these important frameworks more accessible. The goal is that you have "aha" moments in each chapter, and that fresh perspectives help you create more joyful effectiveness in your work with others.

In describing each framework, I have distilled what has been most helpful to me, setting down what I have shared in hundreds of conversations, and drawn on napkins in dozens of cafés. I aim to be true to what I see as the essence of each framework, knowing that others might emphasize different aspects.

If you like what is here, I encourage you to learn more. The Further Resources section recommends books, articles, and websites where you can gain deeper understanding, learn practical next steps, and be inspired by stories and case studies. There are also communities of people engaged in furthering each of the frameworks. Perhaps you will be inspired to join them.

Who should use this book?

This book is for anyone who would like more savvy in relationships, groups, organizations, and any other human system. You do not need to be in a formal leadership position. There are gems here

Frameworks are like maps

About 35 years ago, a friend told me, "Maps are gold." If you are fluent in a variety of "maps" for the territories you want to navigate, then finding your way is easy.

I have to admit that at the time I did not understand what he was talking about. It sounded deep and advanced, but I was too proud to ask him to say more.

I never forgot the comment though, and as I went about my work in social change and community development, I grew to appreciate the value in different maps.

Maps help you see a landscape from different perspectives. A road map shows streets and highways, while a cycling map covers the same territory avoiding steep hills and impassable bridges.

By analogy, different maps of how humans are in groups highlight different "features." Some show how groups evolve over time, and others illuminate power dynamics. Some support innovation, and others highlight the quality of relationships.

Put another way, any framework we use – consciously or unconsciously – helps us see some things, but leaves us blind to others. And this is a critical challenge: whatever is in our blind spot tends to cause us problems.

I have an update to Kurt Lewin's comment, "There is nothing so practical as a good theory." For me, there is nothing so practical as the interplay of several good theories. We get a more complete picture when the blind spots in one framework are illuminated by the different perspectives of other frameworks. (See the following Depth Perception sidebar.)

for you if you are a board member, a frontline worker, a middle manager, or the boss. You might be an entrepreneur, consultant, coach, or parent.

Interacting and working with others such a big part of our lives that we can all benefit from increasing our awareness and skill in navigating collective waters.

You can also benefit from this book if you want to understand yourself better and to grow personally. Indeed, the process of becoming more effective in our collaborative work calls on us to grow personally, and when we grow personally, we automatically become more effective participants in our relationships, groups, teams, and more.

Using this book

Each chapter introduces one framework. You can explore them in order, or jump around. The important thing is to apply the framework to a group you are currently part of, or to one you know well. What does the framework reveal? What questions does it raise?

Once you have even two frameworks under your belt, explore what they have to say to each other. Take them to a café with a colleague, or to the conversation by the water cooler. What do they help you see, and how much richer is the picture when you use two frameworks instead of one?

Keep adding frameworks, working with different pairings for a day or a week. Mix them up. Make them yours. It takes time to integrate ways of seeing, and it stretches us to see things in new ways. But it does not take that long! Once you experience the value in the frameworks you will want to keep them close. You will soon notice that you are using the frameworks automatically – you will have trained yourself to look through different lenses and see dimensions that were previously invisible.

Icons

As support for seeing how the frameworks can work together, there are a few icons sprinkled throughout the book. Each icon represents a specific framework. In the Appreciative Inquiry chapter, for example, there are icons for Generative Dialogue ↻, Theory U ひ and Enterprise Facilitation △.

Of course, there are many other links between the frameworks than the few marked by icons. The goal is to highlight a few connections in the hopes of sparking you to see more.

To know what each icon means, see the Tool Guide at the very end of this book.

The Tool Guide

The Tool Guide offers an overview of how I apply the frameworks to common group situations. My intention is that this book is a resource you come back to again and again, any time you welcome insights into how to move forward in a group context. This brief overview shares which frameworks I am most likely to use for

Depth perception

I first learned about depth perception when I was 12 years old and suffering from conjunctivitis (pink eye). My grandfather was an ophthalmologist, and he recommended letting one eye rest for a day by covering it with a patch. Wow! Suddenly I was bumping into things and had a hard time with stairs.

Try it for yourself right now, by covering one eye with a hand. You will see how everything around you is still there, but "flat" – two dimensional rather than the vivid depth we can see with two eyes.

Working with one framework is like seeing with one eye. While you can see everything, there is not as much depth as when you add in a second framework.

With practice, you will become comfortable seeing groups and organizations with three and more frameworks simultaneously, gaining even greater depth of perspective.

specific circumstances, such as forming a new group, dealing with conflict, or contending with a lack of leadership.

Other suggestions for working with the frameworks

In the chapter called What To Do Monday Morning, two checklists provide an overview of all the frameworks and a sample quick reference of how each framework can support your group work. The goal of this chapter is to help you integrate working with the frameworks on an ongoing basis, in any group situation.

At the personal level

Perhaps the best way to integrate the insights and capacities each lens brings is to **use the tools on ourselves**. In each of the framework chapters, there is a section called "At the personal level", with suggestions for how to use that tool on yourself.

I hope you will take a few minutes to try these suggestions, or to find your own ways to apply the tools at the personal level. That way you will gain embodied knowing of the frameworks so they are at your fingertips in group situations when you need them.

This point is so important I will say it another way: Tools neatly stored in a toolbox are no help. Tools that have helped you grow personally will be more immediately in your lived experience. Having a direct personal experience of their benefits makes it more likely that you will think to use a tool in the flux and tumult of group situations. Moreover, the more the frameworks' complementary perspectives become integrated into how you see the world, the more this will help grow your ability to foster positive outcomes, simply by the quality of your being.

Making Light Work

While I have written *We Can Do This!* to stand alone, it builds on and complements my earlier book, *Make Light Work: 10 Tools for Inner Knowing.*[2] Both books offer simple tools for working with

---

2   Sutherland, Kate. *Make Light Work: 10 Tools for Inner Knowing.* Vancouver, British Columbia: Incite Press, 2010.

the interior dimension. Both are about inner work – ways of working that are based in intention, perception, intuition, and consciousness.

By focusing on frameworks, *We Can Do This!* emphasizes the perception aspect of inner work. Perception then serves as a doorway to intention, intuition, and consciousness. For example, by helping us to see group dynamics more clearly, a framework raises questions, and those questions are opportunities to connect with our intuitive knowing. A framework illuminates issues, and illuminating issues invites us to set conscious intention about how things will unfold. A framework raises awareness of *what is,* and the more conscious awareness we bring to a situation, the more likely we are to create vibrant and dynamic outcomes.

The most important element in both books is an invitation to do our own "Groundwork." Groundwork calls us to bring conscious attention to the quality of being we bring to what we do. It is also the easiest aspect of life to overlook, since we tend to be fixated on *doing* rather than *being. We Can Do This!* includes a chapter on Groundwork that builds on a similar chapter from *Make Light Work.* I hope you will practice Groundwork when working with the frameworks, and indeed, in every aspect of your life. It alone is enough to improve significantly how things play out in groups.

Challenges? Ask for help!

Perhaps the most important piece to integrate is the practice of asking for help. Whenever you face a challenge in your personal life or a group situation, take this as life nudging you to do some form of inner work. It is amazing how things shift and transform when we bring to bear the insights and possibilities from our individual and collective interiors. We have tremendous potential for greater grace and ease in all aspects of our lives, the way many hands make light work of cleaning up after a meal.

Set an intention

To put this into practice immediately, I invite you to pause and reflect on your intentions in reading this book. In writing it, I have set the intention that it helps you bring forth the best in the human systems you are part of. You do not need to be a formal leader or facilitator to have a profound positive impact on group energy and effectiveness.

Perhaps you have different or further intentions. Perhaps you have a specific group in mind. Whatever is most alive for you, take a moment to set your intention for reading consciously. This is a powerful way to get the most out of your time with this book.

And be in touch

We Can Do This! is part of a wider body of work dedicated to helping inner work tools and approaches become as universal as cooking pots. I would love to hear from you. Stories are one of the most powerful ways to transfer knowledge. Your story will be just what someone else needs to hear.

Groundwork

How we are on the inner
affects how things go on the outer.

Before we dive into the tool chapters, I am delighted to introduce Groundwork – perhaps the most important offering in the book. As the name suggests, you can think of Groundwork as laying a foundation – the inner preparation that sets you up for better outcomes when using the frameworks. Without a strong foundation, what we build can be off-kilter or even misguided. With a strong foundation, what you build is more likely to be solid and aligned with life.

Groundwork does not take much time. What it does require is paying attention to things we usually ignore, the way a fish does not see the water it swims in.

Seeing the water

As a kid, my favourite museum was the local Science Centre, and one of the best parts was the Arcade, a huge gallery of games and activities that taught science through play. Every time I was there, I delighted in the optical illusions, seeing first a hag and then a beautiful woman, or first faces, then a vase, and back to faces.

What I loved was the way optical illusions reveal how choice is at the heart of what we see. In the image shown here, do you focus on what is black, or what is white?

If you see the black faces, then white is the ground of what you see, and you miss the vase. If instead you see the white vase, then black is the ground for you, and you miss the two people almost nose to nose. Both are valid ways of seeing, but in our day-to-day lives, we tend to miss "the ground" because we are focused only on what scientists of perception call "the figure."

What if we applied the logic of optical illusions to daily life? What if, for example, we balanced our society's emphasis on *doing* (the figure) with more attention on how we are *being* (the ground)? What if we trained ourselves to see both the "figure" and the "ground" in all situations?

Our inner state

Perhaps you can relate: There you are, with a hammer, wanting to bang in a nail. If you are centered in confidence, patience, and peace, you can sink the nail with relative ease. When you are caught in agitation, impatience, or anger, the same hammer hits your thumb, bends the nail, or dents the wood. The different outcomes reflect the differences in your inner state.

By bringing more attention to this "ground," professional facilitators and consultants have come to speak of "self as instrument." They recognize that how they show up – the quality of being they bring to their work – has tremendous implications for what happens in a group or system.

The same will be true for you as you use the frameworks in this book. If you use the tools to get your way, prove you are right, impress people, or for other ego-based agendas, you will have limited results. If you come from fear, righteousness, or despair the outcomes will also be compromised. Such a version of your "self" will be an ineffective instrument of change.

To get the most from the frameworks, hone your self.

Perhaps this is old hat. You may have seen how your inner state gets magnified in how things unfold in the "outer".

Or, "Yikes!" you might be saying. "I just need some tools to better navigate in my team."

In either case, each of us is a work-in-progress with ragged edges, triggers that track to core wounds from childhood, and dreams we have yet to fulfill. In other words, we are human!

At least once a day and sometimes five times an hour, I see places where I have been blind, or triggered, or played small. When I reflect on those moments, it could be that I wanted approval, or felt I did not belong. C Sometimes I am competing rather than listening, or have closed my heart in judgment of a person or situation.

Remembering my humanity is key. Knowing there is "a crack in everything"[1] – including myself – keeps me honest. It invites me to accept myself exactly as I am, and also to keep working my edges and triggers and dreams.

Holding space

Perhaps you have had the experience of feeling really heard in a way that made it easier for you to speak what was in your heart and mind. Someone held space for you in a way that let you access thoughts and emotions you had not been able to express before.

The same dynamic happens in groups. When there is at least one person in a group who brings depth and awareness, their ability to see and hear from a deeper place makes it easier for others to say what is real and to act authentically.

The frameworks in this book give you ten different perspectives on yourself and any group situation. As you integrate working with them, you will deepen your ability to be that someone in the group who makes it easier for others to show up. ∧

---

1   From Anthem, a beautiful song by master poet and songwriter Leonard Cohen.
    Here is a bit more:
    "Forget your perfect offering
    There is a crack, a crack in everything
    That's how the light gets in"

The more we can both accept our humanity and keep taking the next step in our growth, the more likely we are to have compassion for others. We are all, after all, in the same boat: works in progress, doing our best.

And this, it turns out, makes us much more effective as instruments of change. When we are 'doing our work', as my therapist mother says, the people around us can tell. We have a certain kind of presence – a way of being that comes from self awareness, self acceptance, self honesty, and self compassion.

Doing work on our own issues gives us ground to stand on. It helps us answer the question, "Who am I to intervene in this situation?" No matter our formal position or role in a system, we can know that our own truth has value. From this ground, we humbly try, doing our best to bring a positive contribution.

Two honing practices

The rest of this chapter is about the two most powerful practices I know for quickly and profoundly shifting the quality of being I bring to my life and work. I hope they are as beneficial for you as they have been for me.

First up: Groundwork. Then we will unpack Groundwork a bit more by exploring trust as illuminated by Jack Gibbs's Trust Theory[2].

Many readers of my first books have told me that the Groundwork practice has been their most valuable takeaway, and that they use it to lay a foundation for their day, every day, and often many times a day, whether or not they use any other tools.

The Groundwork practice is equally fundamental to helping groups thrive. Regardless of your position or role, if you do the

---

2   Jack Gibb was an early innovator at the renowned National Training Laboratories (NTL) in Bethel, Maine. There, in the 1940s and 50s, behavioural scientists performed pioneering work in team dynamics, communication, sensitivity training, and leadership training. Gibb was one of the first and most highly regarded training group (T-Group) leaders at NTL and served as its Director of Research. Often referred to as the grandfather of organizational development, Gibb was an internationally acclaimed consultant for such clients as IBM, AT&T, and General Motors. For more on his work, see Jack Gibb. *Trust: A New View of Personal and Organizational Development*, Los Angeles, The Guild of Tutors Press, 1978.

practice before or during a group session, it will contribute to the level of trust and presence and awareness in that group. If others in the group do the practice too, so much the better!

Here's how to do it.

GROUNDWORK

1. Center through self-awareness

If awareness is like a lamp, we tend to spend most of our time illuminating things, people, and ideas around us, and very little time shining light on ourselves.

The moment I bring awareness to my breath, or to my shoulders, or to my core (the solar plexus), it is as if I snap back "home." Other ways to become centered are to meditate, do yoga, chant, sing, go for a walk, or spend time with a tree. Pausing for a moment and simply intending to find your center works too. Being centered is a key foundation for effective work of any kind.

You can proceed to the next step even if you feel upset or out of sorts as long as you are centered enough to be aware of how you are feeling. Being self-aware is synonymous with being centered, even if one is emotionally agitated.

2. Set intention

Once I am centered, I set an overarching intention:

> **"May my work in/with this group serve
> the greatest good for all concerned."**

Sometimes I say, "May I serve what wants to come through." Both phrases are deliberately "big picture." They are not narrowly focused on a specific outcome. I am not saying, for example, "May my work with the group help us win the contract." Rather, I choose words that express my highest aspiration, unconditioned by a specific outcome.

Your words may be different. When you want to connect to your highest aspiration, you might say, "Thy will, not my will." Or "May I serve God or Gaia." A participant at one of my workshops says, "May I serve beauty and truth."

The goal is to find a phrase that shifts your center of gravity away from ego-driven, small "s" self to big "S" Self. It is like flipping a railway switch to take small "s" self off-line and activate big "S" Self, or Soul.

When you find the right words (and these may change over time), you will feel a shift in your awareness. You say or think the phrase and feel more centered, and connected to a greater depth that comes from being in alignment with what matters most.

As I see it, being aligned and serving the highest purpose are two sides of the same coin, and they both require me to be true to life. Alignment means that I am living my purpose, and that my actions, words, thoughts, and energy fulfill my part in the whole.

I am also mindful that I cannot know what outcome would serve the highest purpose. I must approach each situation with humility because my perspective is inevitably limited. Setting an overarching intention is a way of asking that I be guided by life to what is truly of service.

3. Open

After setting intention, the next step is to become open or receptive.

Moment by moment, like clams in a tide pool, we open and close our "shells" – sometimes open, for example, to learning from what a friend has to say, and other times not.

Serving the highest involves being centered in Self enough to be willing to open to other ways of seeing. We only benefit from new frameworks if we are open to the gifts they bring us.

This step involves a moment in which I check in with myself to make sure I am open to new perspectives and insights, and to different ways of doing and being. I have found it helpful to tap into my faith and trust that this is a safe and wonderful thing to do.

Here I often think of a question posed years ago by my brother, Stephen Sutherland: "Is Life your lover or your betrayer?" I think many of us have a foot in each camp. Before using the frameworks, my practice is to "center" myself in the camp where I see life as my lover.

If you are a person who sees life as neither a friend nor a foe, neither good nor evil, the core of this step remains: choose to open to new ways of seeing – and therefore of doing and being.

FIGURE OF EIGHT BREATHING

If you want to center yourself deeply and quickly, try this exercise.

a. Optional: Take off eyeglasses, any heavy jewelry, and footwear made of rubber or plastic.

b. Stand with your feet shoulder width apart, eyes closed, and your attention on your breath. Sitting or lying down works too, but standing is the easiest way to start.

c. Inhale slowly and bring your awareness to your heart.

d. Exhale slowly and imagine your breath is traveling down the front of your body and penetrating to the center of the Earth.

e. Inhale slowly and imagine you are drawing energy up from the center of the Earth, up the back of your body, and into your heart.

f. Exhale slowly and imagine that your breath is going from your heart up the front of your body as high as it can go – to the sky, the stars, heaven – whatever works for you.

g. Inhale slowly and imagine you are drawing energy down from above, down the back of your body and into your heart.

h. Repeat this "figure of eight" as long as feels right – perhaps 5-20 cycles at the beginning. When you are familiar with this practice, four or five cycles is enough to feel quite grounded.

To start, I suggest tracing the figure of eight shape with one hand, as a way to help your awareness move.

Three dials

In practicing Groundwork, it is as though we are adjusting three inner dials: first to centered awareness, second to serving the highest, and third to opening to new perspectives and ways of being. This ground then creates a spaciousness in which we are far more able to be present with *what is* as it unfolds in a group or system.

Try the three steps of the Groundwork practice now. You will know you have done it well when you sense an inner shift: You are coming from a different place. It feels more expansive, grounded, and still. You have tapped into the ground of your being.

Unpacking Groundwork: the choice to trust

Trust Theory helps us unpack the Groundwork practice, especially in the relationship between trust and letting go.

Each of the three steps of the Groundwork practice involve a conscious choice to *let go*.

1. Center through self awareness: Let go of agitation, drama, swirling emotions, and more.

2. Set intention: Let go of small "s" self and control enough to be truly open to what serves the highest good.

3. Open: Let go of control here too, along with beliefs, fears, habitual ways of seeing, judgments, assumptions, being right, and more.

In my experience, letting go is both the easiest thing in the world, and the hardest.

It is easy because there is literally nothing to do. It is a non-doing, similar to the way that having an open hand is effortless compared to making a fist.

It is hard because I hold onto identity, to being right, to having my way. I hold onto my story. I always feel a catch, a clutch in my belly, a hesitation, at the edge of letting go. ∧

This is where trust comes in. Through the practice of *choosing to trust*, I have grown more comfortable with the discomfort of letting go. I have grown the muscle for trust: I choose to trust that, fundamentally, no matter what happens, I will be okay.

Don't get me wrong: there are plenty of times when I am as triggered and agitated as the next person. Sometimes I am lost in the hormonal soup of fight, flight, or freeze. But other times, my "trust muscles" keep me out of the soup, or in it for shorter and shorter dips, thanks to honing my "self" with this practice.

I am not saying you have to let go of everything. For example, I DO hold onto my purpose, values, and principles, but to allow for emergence, I hold them lightly. ⊘

Trust Theory[3]

In case it is as helpful for you as it has been for me, I want to share more about Jack Gibb's Trust Theory.

Here is Trust Theory at its most succinct:

> *Trust and fear are keys to understanding persons and social systems.* They are primary and catalytic factors in all human living.[4]

Imagine a spectrum from extreme fear to total trust. Every individual, group, and organization is operating within a particular range along this continuum. The higher the levels of trust, the more creative, innovative, dynamic, and effective the group or organization will be.

Without trust, it is as if there is no fabric or material to work with. People's perspectives and gifts are locked away, kept off the table and out of mind. In chronically low-trust environments, people "show up" less and less over time. There is an ever-growing gap between what is expressed and what is underneath.

Gibb also offers a powerful four-step model of how trust helps groups of people to thrive. He summarizes the model in the acronym "TORI," which stands for Trust, Openness, Realization, and Interdependence.

---

3   This is a pared down introduction to Trust Theory. For a chapter dedicated to this fabulous framework, go to http://www.katersutherland.com/wp/wp-content/uploads/2017/07/Trust-Theory-Oc9.pdf

4   *Trust*, page 16, italics in the original.

The TORI framework holds that when there is a high level of **Trust**, we are freed up to be ourselves and can drop limiting roles and positions.

Trust naturally leads to **Openness** – information flows between people; people say what they think, know, care about, and need.

Trust and Openness lead to **Realization** – people express and create in ways that are deeply meaningful to them.

When groups have high levels of Trust, Openness, and Realization, they naturally mature into higher levels of **Interdependence** (and community), boundaries blur, and there is ever more synergy and effectiveness.

Moreover, TORI applies to all aspects of the human experience:

> For those of us who use it, the unique quality of TORI (Trust Level) theory comes from its bridging power – the use of a single set of constructs, minimal in number, to apply to all professional tasks and human institutions. The same theory is applied to the total range of human problems: ... from diagnosing the counter culture to understanding the board room at General Motors; from the fear of having the incorrect dress length to existential dread; from child care to international relations; ... The theory's power lies in its effort to apply a single set of basic constructs to a universal range of phenomena.[5]

So how do we cultivate trust?

Gibb has two primary directives:

- Create a high-quality environment – one that supports people to trust.[6]
- Choose to trust yourself in a way that lets you be authentic and role-free.

Going deeper, it turns out that these two directives are actually two sides of the same coin.

---

5 *Trust,* page 18.

6 For more on how to create a high-quality environment, go to http://www.katersutherland.com/wp/wp-content/uploads/2017/07/Trust-Theory-Oc9.pdf

The most powerful lever for creating a high-trust environment lies within each of us: ***Be trusting!*** The more we trust life, ourselves, and the group, the more we create a high-quality environment.

Gibb maintains that such trust is a choice:

> Clear evidence from biofeedback and from more clinical approaches demonstrates that supposedly "involuntary" and "unconscious" processes can be brought under voluntary and conscious control. I give myself my trust and my joy. I create my life. I create my own mindbodyspirit in ways that would once have been discussed only in the wildest fantasies of science fiction.[7]

In other words, we can *choose* to trust both ourselves and our environment. We can shift ourselves out of fear and into trust. Making this choice has a profound effect on how we experience our environment, and it ripples out to affect profoundly how others experience the same environment. There is a contagion effect. Trust begets trust!

I think of it as throwing my hat into the ring, or taking a plunge into the river of life. Moment by moment, I *choose* to trust myself. I am enough. I do not need to take on a role or wear a mask to protect myself and keep myself safe. I do not need to be careful about what I say or do. I can trust what flows through me. I can let myself flow; I can be present and personal.

This trust in one's essential goodness allows you to trust the essential goodness in others. You will not be undone or humiliated. You trust that you can handle whatever happens when you show up as who you really are. It is safe for you to unfold.

The environment is high-trust because you choose to see it that way and act accordingly. Each of us creates our own environment through our internal choices. You can choose to trust, even in unlikely conditions.

The more you can be yourself, trusting that it is safe for you to show up without leaving any part of yourself behind, the more you create safety for others to do the same. In this way, regardless

---

7 *Trust*, page 69.

of your formal role in a situation, you can have a powerful impact on groups.

When I drop the "role" of group facilitator, for example, paradoxically I am much more able to support groups to be effective. I find the same thing as a parent, coach, and instructor. It is as if my stepping out from behind a cardboard cut-out sends a signal that others can do the same. By this modelling, I wordlessly invite others to join me in coming from and opening to the ever deeper ground of our being.

In Summary

I hope you will keep exploring the endless gifts of both the three-step Groundwork practice, and the moment by moment practice of choosing to trust. Together, they set in motion a wonderful cascade that will both benefit you personally and deepen your ability to support transformative change in the relationships, groups, and human systems you care about.

For me, honing our "self as instrument" with these two Groundwork practices is the most fundamental contribution that each of us can make to the groups we are part of. If I had to choose between doing Groundwork and using the ten frameworks that follow, I would choose Groundwork every time. The benefits are so profound.

Thankfully, there is no need to choose. We can have both: lay the foundation of our quality of being AND receive the benefit of the frameworks for making decisions, forming new organizations, dealing with conflict – you name it.

1
Appreciative Inquiry

Focus on possibilities, not problems.

I love each of the frameworks in this book, so it has been like planning a delicious meal for much loved friends to choose which "dish" to serve first. I have picked Appreciative Inquiry because it offers a brilliant entry point to virtually every context, and because it is simple and stunningly transformational. I also welcome how it infuses everything with a joyous sweetness. When we appreciate something, not only does it help us amplify what we have appreciated, we, the appreciators, are uplifted and energized and connected to our wisdom and passion.

At the core of Appreciative Inquiry's transformational power is one of the most fundamental inner shifts we can make: from seeing problems to seeing possibilities.

Most of us, and most groups, tend to focus on what is wrong. We relish cataloguing what is not working and we glory in analyzing root causes and how things might get worse.

The same is true for the voices in our heads. "You didn't do that very well." "Don't be so stupid." "Who do you think you are?" Seldom does our self-talk affirm our strengths or honour our accomplishments.

All this negative focus is debilitating. The bigger the problems we face and the more overwhelmed we are by the weight of what is wrong, the more important it is that we shift our focus to seeing what is right.

Appreciative Inquiry is an approach to life and to working in groups that turns our default-setting on its head. Instead of fixating on problems, the focus is on what is life-giving. The shift is that simple, and the implications are profound – for morale, innovation, creativity, getting things done, and more. See the following Bright Spots sidebar for one vivid example.

Origins

Appreciative Inquiry began with David Cooperrider and Suresh Srivastva at Case Western University. In 1980, Cooperrider, then 24, was a doctoral student of Organizational Behavior. While conducting a standard (problem-focused) diagnosis of organizational issues at a Cleveland clinic, Cooperrider was amazed by the positive cooperation, goodwill, and innovation that he found among the staff. Encouraged by Srivastva, his academic supervisor, Cooperrider dug deeper into what excited him, and gained permission from the clinic to do a thorough investigation of the factors in play when the clinic was functioning at its best. The results were so positive that the clinic's board of directors extended the work to the whole group practice. The term "appreciative inquiry" first appeared as a footnote in a report to the clinic by Cooperrider and Srivastva.

In the 37+ years since then, thousands of people have built on this and each other's work, teasing out principles and practices, and generously sharing stories and insights, united by a focus on the bright spots.[1]

---

1 Learn more about the history and developments in Appreciative Inquiry at the Appreciative Inquiry Commons website. See Further Resources.

Appreciative lens

Appreciative Inquiry focuses on the "positive core" – the factors and characteristics that are present when an individual, group, organization, or community is at its best.

By asking, "what do you value?," or "what works well here?" – even in the most toxic of communities, workplaces, or teams – the conversation changes in profound ways. ⟳ The appreciative focus surfaces people's wisdom and goodwill. In place of negativity, despair, and overwhelm, people's latent decency, wisdom, and engagement are unleashed. Authentic appreciation, and its close cousin, gratitude, shift the energy. For both individuals and groups, that energy shift is like wind in the sails for positive change.

Bright spots

A focus on the bright spots allowed a foreign aid worker to greatly improve child nutrition in Vietnam in a mere six months and with zero budget for food. Instead of focusing on the malnourished children, his team located families where babies had above average weight, a direct indicator of better nourishment. The researchers culled out those families that had higher than average incomes, to leave only families with babies doing better than average given their family circumstances. Then local research assistants investigated what these families were doing differently. It turned out that the differences were simple and highly replicable: in place of two to three larger meals, the bright spot families were feeding the same amount of food per day in four to five smaller portions, and they were supplementing their children's diets with readily available weeds (greens), and small shrimp wild harvested from the rice paddies. By organizing meetings where the bright spot mothers shared with other mothers the specifics of what they were doing, the innovations spread quickly – significantly and quickly improving the nutrition of local children.[2]

---

2 Adapted from Switch: *How to change when change is hard*, by Chip Heath and Dan Heath. Crown Business, 2010.

Inquiry

Energized by having discovered something to appreciate, the next questions become, "What are the conditions that supported this wonderful thing to happen? How can we have more of what is working? Can we translate what is working *here* to help us over *there*?"

Inquiry helps us understand how the "bright spots" came to be, and points the way to having many more.

What conditions, for example, contributed to the best meeting you have ever had with your team or board or staff? Was the agenda framed in a positive and inspiring way? Was everyone comfortable to say what was real, thanks to a high level of trust? Was there a dynamic cross-section of people participating? Did it start on an upbeat note?

Looking back at times when your company or organization was performing at its best, was there excellent information flow between sub-groups, or a compelling sense of shared purpose, or people supported to try new things?

If your goal is to help team members to be more punctual, or better informed, or more engaged, get curious about the people who are already punctual, informed, and engaged. Or ask team members to reflect on their best experiences of whatever you want to cultivate. The wisdom on how to have more will be in the group, △ and when people come up with their own solutions, they are far more likely to implement them.

At the personal level

Over time, working appreciatively becomes a way of being. We change our default setting from focusing on what is wrong to seeing what is right. The more we do this in our personal lives, the better we are able we to respond appreciatively in our relationships, groups, and organizations.

2 LOOK INTO WHAT IS **WORKING** AND LIFE GIVING

4 LOOK FOR THE CONDITIONS THAT SUPPORT WHAT WORKS, **AND BUILD ON THEM**

APPRECIATIVE INQUIRY

★ IT'S ALL ABOUT SEEING. ★

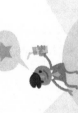

1 SHIFT FROM SEEING **PROBLEMS** TO SEEING **POSSIBILITIES**

3 FOCUS ON WHAT **IS WORKING**

In our personal lives, an appreciative focus can include how we see:

- ourselves;
- our parents and siblings;
- our children;
- our neighbours;
- our circumstances;
- our potential;
- and so on.

Take a moment right now to reflect briefly on some aspect of your personal life from an appreciative perspective. Pick something that is challenging or difficult, and let yourself "rip" with complaining, blaming, or negativity. Then choose to shift from seeing problems to seeing possibilities. Do you notice a shift in your energy and outlook? For example, I recently shifted feeling overwhelmed by my workload into feeling excited by and grateful for emerging possibilities and all that I am learning.

Similarly, in the group and organizational aspects of our lives, bringing an appreciative lens has profound impact. Consider framing issues appreciatively when:

- defining the agenda for a meeting, workshop, conference or social movement;
- conducting a performance review;
- setting strategic goals;
- building capacity in teams and organizations;
- creating collaborations and partnerships;
- dealing with crises.

The list of potential applications is endless because focusing on what is life-giving is a stance we take toward all of life. It is a way of being as much as it is a way of doing. As such, we can bring an appreciative lens to virtually everything!

Since most of us are conditioned by the prevailing negativity and problem focus in society, it takes a bit of practice to strengthen the appreciative "muscle." If you want to be more focused on what is life-giving, you might ask for help from your spouse or a workmate, or you could put a note in your daytimer to explore using the appreciative lens on a daily or weekly basis until you have formed a positive habit.

Another idea is to adapt the Four Ds framework below to your personal or group context.

The Four Ds

In 1990, the Global Excellence in Management Initiative articulated a four-phase framework for working appreciatively in a group context. The framework is called "the Four "D"s, because the key word for each phase starts with the letter "D." Results of working with the Four Ds are best when all parts of the system are together, or well represented – everyone from the boss to the mail room clerk – because wholeness weaves connections and builds trust.

Here are the Four Ds in a nutshell:

- Discover – Who are we at our best? What is working well, and why?

- Dream – Encouraged and inspired by what is already working, what more would we like to see? What is the best outcome we can imagine?

- Design – What steps do we need to take to have our best possible outcome?

- Deliver – Who will do what inspired actions, by when, and what support do they need?

Try the Four Ds in your personal life, to help you improve your fitness, take more risks, or strengthen a key relationship. Try the framework in a team, shifting the conversation from what is not working to looking for bright spots. Let the framework inform your approach if you work on the big issues, such as homelessness, poverty, violence, and war. What are the bright spots? How can we have more of them? ↻

In my experience, an appreciative lens always brings value, whether in a business or community setting, at work or at home. Here is a story about the benefits of an appreciative lens where the outlook was bleak. The storyteller is Glen Griggs, a registered clinical counsellor and consultant.

Appreciative Inquiry in Action

I was once part of a team at a treatment center working with small children who had experienced repeated violence and abuse, and who lived in one of the most economically distressed neighbourhoods in the city. Each of the kids had suffered early peer rejection and academic failure, and had multiple diagnoses, such as post-traumatic stress, dyslexia, inability to sequence, poor impulse control ... They were sponges for discouragement.

The treatment team got together three times a week to coordinate how we did our therapy work, and to keep up morale. We knew about the importance of being appreciative with our clients, and also ourselves. One of the things we appreciated about the team was our willingness to do things that had never been done before: standard treatment protocols were meaningless in this context.

We also paid close attention any time one of us said something like, "The reality is that this child is so reactive he'd never work on changing that behaviour." Whenever someone said, "The reality is ...," we saw this as a signal that our team member's imagination had shutdown, and also as a call to bring creativity to bear.

We made it part of the group culture to reframe those situations. Instead of, "The reality is ...," we'd say, "The current limit of my imagination is ..." So instead of saying,

> "The reality is this family is so disorganized, I can't ever see them getting their kids clean, dressed, and to school on time."

We'd say,

> "The current limit of my imagination is that this family is so disorganized, I can't ever see them getting their kids clean, dressed, and to school on time."

The reframe gave us space to move, space for inquiry. We knew that if we did not work with creativity and possibility, the only alternative was a downward spiral of more and more control and failure.

In the disorganized family, everyone on the team agreed that the family wanted to get their kids to school clean, dressed, and on time – a huge strength to appreciate and build on. What worked in the end was breaking the process down into seven steps, and posting a photograph for each step along the hallway at home. A written list would not have worked for the illiterate parents. The photographs were of the family members themselves, doing steps like waking up the children, the children getting washed ... Seeing themselves doing each step, and having a simple way to remember the sequence, made it possible for the family to do what we previously couldn't have imagined. It would have been even better if the family had taken the photographs themselves, but I did not think of that until just now.

As another example, once a girl stormed out of a therapy session, got on a bus, and went across town. When she later phoned and was picked up, we wanted to know how she did it. This was a child who the week before had been so lacking in confidence that she was not able to open her mouth in the group. In running away, she demonstrated autonomous goal-setting, courage, and strong social skills – to be able to get the bus driver to let her onto the bus without a ticket.

Our goal was to help her develop the confidence and social skills to live life independently. This clarity of purpose automatically changed the meaning of every act of "deviance." Instead of calling us to exert tighter control on her behaviour, we worked to help her value and build on the strengths she had demonstrated. And then to meet the requirement of keeping her safe, we let her know that the next time she wanted to take off, she should ask for a lunch and bus fare, and to go with a friend.

There are dozens more stories of how an appreciative lens helped us work with creativity and possibility in extremely challenging circumstances. Many of them include how team members needed each other's help when we hit the limits of our imagination.

This story demonstrates the potent impact of framing issues appreciatively in tough situations. It is this power that has caused the Appreciative Inquiry lens to be taken up by thousands of people worldwide and from every sector, generating a large body of experience and wisdom I encourage you to explore (see Appreciative Inquiry section in Further Resources). From my own 25+ years of experience and what I have learned from reflecting with others, here are finer points I have found most helpful, and one possible pitfall to avoid.

Finer points

- How issues and challenges are framed is one of the most important places to bring an appreciative lens. For example, from my perspective, the "war on drugs" has actually created more of what it is trying to eliminate. What if the same resources and energy were allocated to cultivating the capacity of families and communities to nurture empowered, confident, self-actualizing youth?

- Appreciative Inquiry is often misunderstood to mean "focus only on the positive." A more helpful approach is to ask, "What is generative?," meaning, "What is life-giving? What creates new possibilities? What is exciting? What is empowering and dynamic?" The shift from "positive" to "generative" helps keep Appreciative Inquiry out on the edge of what is possible rather than playing safe in the nice-y, nice-y politeness backwaters.

- An appreciative lens deals with problems indirectly by inviting people to focus on what they want more of and to dream about ideal futures. Sometimes certain people are concerned that key issues are being shoved under the carpet. They feel that unless problems are tackled head on, there will not be positive change. In these situations, encourage problem-focused people to define what successfully addressing the problem will look like. Invite them to imagine a vivid, comprehensive picture of what life looks like (note the present tense) without the problem. Then encourage them to appreciate even the tiniest step in the right direction, including what already exists. As Lynne Twist says, "What we appreciate appreciates." Alternatively, "What we resist persists."

- Telling appreciative stories is central to the practice and power of Appreciative Inquiry. Stories affirm what is possible, transfer tremendous amounts of knowledge, build relationships, open space for dreaming about what might be, and help us have energy and passion for making a difference.

Sharing stories also leverages the transformative power of listening. When we have a chance to tell a story about something we value to a partner who gives us their openhearted and undivided attention, we often make connections and have deeper insights into experiences that have shaped us. The high quality of listening draws us forth, and at the same time helps to build connections and trust between the teller and the listener. ↻

Try an Appreciative Inquiry interview (see following sidebar, Appreciative Interview Exercise) with a friend to get a sense of what is possible. Pick a subject that matches your purpose ☺ (e.g. best experience in a team for team building, or a time when you were courageous if your goal is to identify core values). The exercise in the sidebar takes 20-30 minutes – and longer if you want to debrief themes and highlights in a larger group. Either way, expect the level of energy and engagement to go up!

Appreciative Interview Exercise

1. Consider what theme will be engaging and enlivening for you or your group to explore. It might be a theme you did not have enough time for in a previous meeting, or that relates to a current goal or issue. Tried and true themes include being courageous, taking a risk, living on purpose, making a difference, feeling alive, and feeling connected to nature.

2. In advance, prepare worksheets or a flip chart with three questions:

a. The theme question. Have this start with, "Tell me a story about ... (for example) a time you came through a major transition."
   b. What conditions supported you to have this experience?
   c. What was the impact of this experience on you, on others, and on your community/world?

3. Introduce the idea of appreciative interviews – how the approach is based on the premise that organizations and people change in the direction in which they inquire. When we inquire into problems, we will keep finding problems, but when we appreciate what is best in ourselves or a situation, we will discover more and more that is good. We can then use these discoveries to build a new future where the best becomes more common. (1-2 minutes)

4. Start by inviting people to take a few minutes of quiet reflection on the theme, recalling a related experience where they felt fully alive. Encourage them to trust what comes to mind. Often a seemingly "small" story expresses deep and important truths. (2-3 minutes)

5. Invite people to partner with someone they do not know well. Once everyone has a partner, ask the pairs to decide who will be Person A and who will be Person B. Let them know that each person will have 7-10 minutes to share their story. Explain that Person A is the interviewer, and encourage them to open their ears and hearts to Person B. A's role is to listen appreciatively and to ask supplementary questions that support Person B to tell their story. (This is not about commenting, or sharing similar experiences, but active listening to support Person B to explore the theme.) While listening, Person A also records themes and key words from what Person B says. Person A starts the interview by saying, "Tell me a story of a time when ...." Once Person B has shared his/her story, Person A asks questions 2 and 3 (from the flipchart). (7-10 minutes)

6. Switch roles. (7-10 minutes)

7. After both interviews, invite pairs to take a few minutes to reflect together on what the exercise was like. (2-3 minutes)

8. OPTIONAL: Debrief in the whole circle.

- Try "provocative propositions" as a great way to shift conversations to be more appreciative. A provocative proposition distills a desired future into a single statement that expands our sense of possibility. ⟲

For example, once I was asked to help a community address child hunger. Rather than convening conversations about hungry children, we worked with the provocative proposition: *"There is food on EVERY table."* This statement contains an inspiring vision that spawned ten projects, all of which supported greater food security for vulnerable families.

Here are other examples of how issues can be framed as provocative propositions.

Typical Frame	Provocative Proposition
Lack of leadership	We lead with passion, power, and purpose. △
Poor communication	The internal and external flows of information and knowledge nourish every part of the organization/ team/company.
Lack of funding	Through partnerships, innovation, and collaboration, we have the resources we need to do excellent work.
Overwhelm	We take care of what is most important and the rest takes care of itself.

It is energizing when we frame issues as a positive, present time statement or question. Take a moment now to write a provocative proposition for an issue in your life – or create one with a buddy, or in your team as a whole.

Possible pitfall

- If senior management is fixed in deficit-based and problem-focused approaches, it is unlikely that they will be authentically committed to acting on the energy and ideas unleashed through an appreciative inquiry. In such situations, it is possible for an appreciative approach to debilitate or demoralize the people involved due to lack of follow through. Look for opportunities to create small successes through working appreciatively, and then build on those successes.

Links to other chapters

As you read the coming chapters, discover for yourself how all the frameworks are either fundamentally appreciative, or that they are greatly enhanced when approached appreciatively. For example, you will see how Enterprise Facilitation is based on what is life-giving, building on where there is passion and capacity, and that Theory U recommends investigating bright spots to learn from what is already working well.

There is a particularly potent link between Appreciative Inquiry and Chaordic Design – the next framework: an appreciative approach helps us to have the vision, passion and energy for creating new, more "chaordic" ways of working together! Often, in groups, it is as if the fabric holding us together is too thin or frail for the group to tackle the real issues/dynamics. To work effectively together, we often need to rethink how we are organized and what we hold as our central purpose. In those instances, an appreciative approach is very helpful. When we reframe problems as possibilities, and when we connect with each other through stories about bright spots and what we value, we weave stronger connections with one another. In these and many other ways, an appreciative approach helps to tap the gifts of working "chaordically".

Questions

The best way to learn more about the appreciative lens is to jump in and try it. Here are questions you might explore by writing in a journal or having a conversation with a learning partner. These are also questions to come back to any time you want a quick way into the appreciative lens:

- Tell me the story of a time you were:
  - courageous;
  - in major transition;
  - contributing in ways you value;
  - playing a leadership role;
  - enthusiastically engaged ...

- What works well here? What is life-giving? What is inspiring? Name one thing that we are doing really well.

- How can we have more of what is working?

- What do I value in myself, in this person, in this context? Who am I at my best? Who are we at our best?

- What is an appreciative question or provocative proposition that will help unleash the potential for positive change in this context?

- How can we reframe this problem? Imagine what our situation looks like without this problem.

- How can we translate what is working for one issue/department/situation to help us with other issues/departments/situations?

2
Chaordic Design

Purpose and principles clearly articulated, deeply understood and commonly shared are the genetic code of any healthy organization. To the degree that purpose and principles are deeply held in common, command and control can be dispensed with. People will know how to behave in accordance with them, and they'll do it in thousands of unimaginable, creative ways. The organization will then become a vital, living set of beliefs and effective action in accordance with them.

Dee Hock[1]

When I first read about Chaordic Design, I had a sense of coming home. What resonated most for me is Chaordic Design's focus on purpose: what are we really trying to do? Clarifying purpose has been my starting point for everything for as long as I can remember. So it was deeply joyful to discover a framework that honours this foundation, and then builds on it – setting out five more steps, each as important and transformational as the first.

In all kinds of contexts, I have found that clarifying and artic- ulating purpose frees people up to make decisions and take things

---

1   Quoted with permission from Dee Hock, creator of Chaordic Design, and former CEO of VISA.

forward. Projects and initiatives become nimble and self-organizing. There is room to run with ideas and passion, and at the same time everyone is enough on the same page for there to be synergy and coherence.

Chaordic Design is also versatile and rigorous. It has guided me in everything from parenting to creating meetings to designing regional change initiatives. I appreciate that this framework calls for seamless coherence between what we are doing and how we do it. It has helped me have courage to stand firm in the face of entrenched interests, and to overcome the inertia of the status quo.

Perhaps the greatest gift of Chaordic Design is as a road map for re-envisioning our institutions and organizations. In this time of massive institutional failure where there are no simple answers, Chaordic Design can guide us in redesigning human systems to be win-win-win for people, our endeavours, and the planet.

Purpose versus vision

Group processes such as strategic planning often include visioning as a way of rekindling passion, setting direction, and getting everyone on the same page. Visioning is very powerful.

Chaordic Design is in the same arena, but different. Purpose is like a guiding question. A group's vision is more like an answer.

Both purpose and vision are important, and can be complementary. For example, you might first get really clear on your purpose, and then do a visioning process!

Chaordic Design

Chaordic Design starts with the question, "What is our shared purpose?"

It is a deceptively simple question, and a crucial one. Humans have a tendency to lose sight of the big picture, and to be preoccupied (happily or unhappily) with plans and actions that are a continuation of the status quo, and too often sub-optimal, misdirected, or downright destructive.

It is important that our time, energy, and resources take us closer to where we want to go. So ask this question at the beginning of a new initiative, or when taking stock along the way: *What is at the core of the core of what we intend?* Or more informally: *What are we trying to do?*

Groups tend to want to jump past this conversation about purpose into strategizing, fixing, action planning, or problem-solving. It takes discipline to slow down ↺ the conversation long enough to support reflection. A true Chaordic Design exploration of organizational purpose can take multiple conversations over weeks or months and even years.

Clarifying a robust and grounded statement of shared purpose is a powerful way to support success. Once Purpose is established and agreed upon, a group can continue with some or all of the next five steps of Chaordic Design: Principles, Participants, Organizational Concept, Constitution, and Practices. Doing so supports the group's functional integrity.

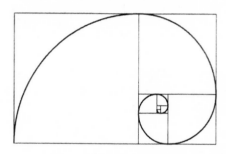

Chaordic Design is often represented with a Fibonacci spiral (see diagram) to express how its six steps help to create a stable pattern. This pattern brings enough structure to allow for growth (in an ever widening spiral), while staying true to the central/founding impulse or purpose.

For 45+ years, working "chaordically" has helped shape optimal human systems at every level, from as small-scale as a single meeting to as large-scale as the design of global corporations.

Origins

Dee Hock pioneered Chaordic Design while creating the VISA credit card clearing system in the late 1960s and 70s. He had had a lifelong passion for creating institutions that do what they set out to do. Why, he had wondered, does our criminal justice system create criminals? Why do schools fail to create engaged and effective citizens? Why do our health care institutions fail to cultivate healthy lifestyles?

In 1965, Hock was working for the National Bank of Commerce right when it and many other financial institutions across the United States were introducing credit cards and jockeying for dominance in what promised to be a lucrative market. For retailers and banks alike, the result was highly chaotic. For example, a single retail outlet could have customers with credit cards from dozens of different financial institutions. Reconciling and clearing all these transactions was a time consuming nightmare, as was the potential for fraud in the time lag between making and processing credit card sales.

Hock saw it as a situation of intense competition with enormous potential benefits from collaboration. It was also a challenging test case for a different type of institution building.

You can read the story[2] of how Hock led development of the VISA credit card clearing system, a radically different kind of organization, which is now global in scope and facilitates trillions of dollars in transactions. Hock's story makes for a riveting read, full of twists and Herculean feats. It also offers an inspiring template for the renewal and re-imagination of human institutions.

VISA is different

Often, when Dee Hock was invited to speak, he would hold up a VISA card and ask who recognized it. Hands would shoot up. Then he would ask if anyone could say who owns VISA, who governs VISA, where it is headquartered, or how to buy shares. Typically, there would be confused silence.

Rather than the traditional models of corporate ownership and top-down control, Hock explained, "VISA has elements of Jeffersonian democracy, it has elements of the free market, of government franchising – almost every kind of organization you can think about. But it's none of them. Like the body, the brain, and the biosphere, it's largely self-organizing."[3]

---

2   See *Birth of the Chaordic Age*, 1999, by Dee Hock, Berrett-Koehler Publishers, Inc.,San Francisco, CA. www.bkconnection.com

3   Source: Dee Hock. Quoted with permission.

"Chaord" and "chaordic"

Hock believes the main reason so many human systems fail to achieve their intended purpose is excessive order: rules, regulations, procedures, and policies entangle and stifle human initiative.[4] On the other hand, too little structure (chaos) is similarly inhibiting of effective collective endeavour.

The goal, in his view, is to find the optimal balance of *chaos* and *order*. He coined the word "chaordic"[5] to express this balance: the band along the spectrum between order and chaos where social systems are dynamic and effective, and people thrive. (See the illustration on page 51.)

The big question is: how? How can we create companies, institutions, and organizations that are "chaordic"?

Hock identified the six dimensions – from Purpose to Practice – of a process now known as Chaordic Design. It has since been embraced by leaders, innovators, consultants, and facilitators the world over.

We will go into each aspect in more detail, but first, here is the story of a successful change initiative at a conservative Dutch-based bank, thanks, in part, to the Chaordic framework. Think what could happen if more workplaces followed in their footsteps.

Chaordic Design in action

In 2003, two colleagues at the bank wanted to make positive change. One worked in the Human Resources Department; the

---

4   According to Dee Hock, "Institutions should enable people but at present, they are disabling. Everywhere I go I ask workers, 'how much of your time do you spend circumventing stupid rules and ridiculous demands that have nothing to do with what you were hired to perform?' Rarely do I hear 'under 50 percent.' The truth is that most people are spending most of their energy and ingenuity circumventing the organization of which they are a part." Quoted with permission from Dee Hock.

5   Chaordic is "the behavior of any self-governing organism, organization or system which harmoniously blends characteristics of order and chaos." A **chaord** is "any self-organizing, self-governing, adaptive, nonlinear, complex organism, organization, community or system, whether physical, biological or social, the behavior of which harmoniously blends characteristics of both chaos and order." Reprinted with permission of the publisher. From *Birth of the Chaordic Age*, 1999 by Dee Hock, Berrett-Koehler Publishers, Inc.,San Francisco, CA. All rights reserved. www.bkconnection.com

other had the "Sustainability" brief. They met sharing a common question: how can this bank be a vehicle for positive change in the world?

Their first move was to invite bank employees to a meeting to share perspectives on "What are you passionate about? What legacy would you like to leave in the world?" To their delight, 75 people showed up from all corners – across departments, generations, and genders, and from bottom to top of the hierarchy.

With this strong response, and thanks to high-level champions, the original pair brought in two consultants to support employees in co-creating what soon gelled as a "Personal Leadership and Change Community." Informed by Chaordic Design, a small group of co-workers worked through the steps to form the Change Community, ensuring it cut across organizational silos.

Listening for what had attracted people (the need), the group framed the Change Community's core purpose:

"To live, plant, and support action at [the bank] towards more meaningful and inspiring work/life."

They also identified ten guiding principles, including:

- We are nourished by successes and mistakes along our way.
- We support and inspire each other.
- We investigate and connect to other initiatives in [the bank] of a similar intent.

The group was not a department. It had no formal leader, and no budget. Instead it offered "spaces" – an intranet site, monthly circles, and quarterly World Café or Open Space[6] events – where people were invited to share their ideas and dreams and to find others to join them in taking action.

The Change Community became the "go to" place for people with an idea, and spawned initiatives ranging from events and programs all the way to policy change for the bank as a whole.

---

6   Open Space Technology is an approach to meeting design where topics and conversation convenors emerge from participants in the group process, rather than being pre-determined by event organizers.

Taking stock after five years, the Change Community proudly articulated their successes. These points show how a chaordic process is alive and enlivening, activating people, and unleashing passion and contribution. Notice how it kindled individuals, relationships, collaborations, innovation, creativity, forward thinking, and resilience.

Benefits to the business we saw ...

- Nurturing internal innovation capabilities
- Shaping and igniting leadership capacities
- Engaging across diverse business units, functions, and cultures
- Developing design and hosting skills
- Attracting and motivating key employees
- Activating dialogue
- Expanding imagination and generating creative solutions
- Exploring and responding to tomorrow's opportunities
- Developing collaborative potential
- Experiencing intergenerational discussion and wisdom
- Building trust, relationships, and accountability
- Fostering internal personal and institutional resiliency

Looking back on the whole process, Tatiana Glad, one of the consultants, highlights how supporting change agents fosters organizational and societal change. When the purpose is to make a difference, beneficial initiatives can come from anywhere in a system. Chaordic Design is a powerful framework for creating an environment that nurtures and connects change makers, whether for an organization as a whole, or for a self-selecting community within a larger context, as in the Dutch bank.

The process was not without challenges. It bumped into organizational bureaucracy, hierarchy, slow decision-making, and the tension between one's formal job description and informal time spent adding value to the whole. However, the Change Community was also a space where people could bring such tensions and benefit from support and collective intelligence about ways to navigate the system.

> In this particular story, a 2009 merger swept in new management. There was no longer high-level support for the Change Community and there ceased to be monthly meetings. But the genie was out of the bottle. The ripples had made changes in 45 departments of the bank. The new skills and experience of working "chaordically" cannot help but be part of ongoing stories of everyone involved. In fact, several of these Change Community members are now entrepreneurs using the Chaordic framework in designing their new ventures.

In addition to demonstrating the ripple effects of Chaordic Design, the above story shares a great way to get started: create what is called a "parallel organization." Parallel organizations are relatively easy to get underway in that you build something new right alongside an existing organization. Typically, parallel organizations include a representative slice of the whole organization, and have only as much structure as needed and no more. This helps innovation and change to flourish as people's ideas and passion are free to flow relatively unencumbered by turf, policies, and protocols.

Using Chaordic Design

According to Hock, the Chaordic Design process can start by asking a fundamental question: "If anything imaginable is possible, if there are no constraints whatever, what would be the nature of an ideal organization to ...?"[7] How we finish this question is crucial. What are we really trying to do? The openness and freedom in the first part of Hock's question is most generative when it is applied to a specific and meaningful purpose. ↻

Before going further, take a moment to think of a current goal or initiative where fresh perspective might be helpful. I recommend starting with something small, like a phone call or other simple task. This will help you experience Chaordic Design as a framework applicable to all sorts of situations in addition to it being an approach to organization building.

---

7   Reprinted with permission of the publisher. From Birth of the Chaordic Age,1999 by Dee Hock, Berrett-Koehler Publishers, Inc., San Francisco, CA. All rights reserved. www.bkconnection.com, page 7.

The following sections introduce each of the six steps in Chaordic Design and suggest some sample associated questions.

1. Purpose

Purpose is like a seed. Everything that unfolds comes from purpose. A slight change in the framing of shared purpose creates significant change in all that follows. For this reason, it is important to delve deeply into what is at the core of shared purpose.

An effective statement of purpose will be a clear, commonly understood statement of that which identifies and binds the community together as worthy of pursuit. When properly done, it can usually be expressed in a single sentence. Participants will say about the purpose, "If we could achieve that, my life would have meaning.[8]

Questions

- What is our shared purpose? What are we here to do, really?
- What is at the core of what we intend?
- What is specific and defining about what we intend?
- What is the simplest and most powerful question we could keep at the core of our work?

2. Principles

Once the purpose has been clearly stated, the next step is to define, with the same clarity, conviction and common understanding, the principles by which those involved will be guided in pursuit of that purpose. Principles typically have high ethical and moral content, and developing them requires engaging the whole person, not just the intellect. The best will be descriptive, not prescriptive, and each principle will illuminate the others. Taken as a whole, together with the purpose, the principles constitute the body of belief that will bind the community together and against which all decisions and acts will be judged.[9]

---

8 Quoted with email permission from Dee Hock.
9 Quoted with email permission from Dee Hock.

Hock is clear that Chaordic principles go far beyond platitudes; the principles, among other things, must tackle the locus of power and the distribution of rewards.

See the textbox below for some of the principles that guided the creation of VISA, where the goal was to support a self-organizing system characterized by both competition and collaboration. Hock's working group spent months defining and gaining acceptance of a set of principles. They became the clear-cut criteria he used for evaluating the moves and countermoves of many high-powered stakeholders. When strong winds are blowing, clarity of purpose and principles help you stay on course.

Questions

- What principles follow from our purpose?
- What principles best guide the locus of decision making and the allocation of rewards?
- What can we not compromise?
- What pressure can we anticipate – and what principles best guide our response to these pressures?

Sample chaordic principles for VISA[10]

- It should be open to all qualified participants.
- Power, function, and resources should be distributive to the maximum degree.
- To the maximum degree possible, everything should be voluntary.
- It should be infinitely malleable yet extremely durable.

---

3. Participants

The next step is to identify everyone who is touched by the purpose and principles. Typically, this will involve a wider definition

---

10 Reprinted with permission of the publisher. From *Birth of the Chaordic Age,*1999 by Dee Hock, Berrett-Koehler Publishers, Inc.,San Francisco, CA. All rights reserved. www.bkconnection.com, pages 138-9.

of stakeholders than previously considered. Being inclusive of more perspectives and interests increases the quality of the design.

Questions

- Who has a stake in our purpose?
- What groups and individuals have an interest, need, or perspective relevant to our purpose?
- Which stakeholders do our principles call us to invite into this process? ∧

4. Organizational concept

When all relevant and affected parties have been identified, drafting team members creatively search for and develop a general concept for the organization. In the light of purpose and principles, they seek innovative organizational structures that can be trusted to be just, equitable, and effective with respect to all participants, in relation to all practices in which they may engage. They often discover that no existing form of organization can do so and that something new must be conceived.[11]

Questions

- What ownership structures reflect and serve our purpose, principles, and participants?
- How will we make decisions?
- How will we ensure we stay on track? How are our structures likely to play out over time?

5. Constitution

Once the organizational concept is clear, the details of organizational structure and functioning are expressed in the form of a written constitution and by-laws. These documents will incorporate, with precision, the substance of the previous steps. They will embody purpose, principles and concept, specify rights, obligations and relationships

---

11 Quoted with email permission from Dee Hock.

of all participants, and establish the organization as a legal entity under appropriate jurisdiction.[12]

Questions

- Are we articulating the structure in a way that is clear and robust?
- Is anything missing in the constitution?
- Is the constitution "chaordic"? Are we true to our purpose, principles, and participants?

6. Practices

With clarity of shared purpose and principles, the right participants, an effective concept and a clear constitution, practices will naturally evolve in highly focused and effective ways. They will harmoniously blend cooperation and competition within a transcendent organization trusted by all. Purpose is then realized far beyond original expectations, in a self-organizing, self-governing system capable of constant learning and evolution.[13]

Questions

- What practices naturally follow from all our design work?
- What is working well? + What are our challenges?
- What are we learning? How can we incorporate what we are learning?
- Are we still true to our purpose, principles, and participants?

You may notice, as I do, that of the six steps (Purpose, Principles, People, Concept, Constitution and Practices), the first two or three are what you draw on most often.

Again, give Chaordic Design a try with something small, like a single meeting or small task. You can either share the framework with others involved, or work through it on your own. Either way, what follow are finer points and possible pitfalls to help along the way.

---

12 Quoted with email permission from Dee Hock.
13 Quoted with email permission from Dee Hock.

Finer points

- Groundwork, is profoundly chaordic. ○ When we set the intention to be of service, whichever way we express that for ourselves, we lay a foundational purpose to make the best possible contribution for all concerned. In other words, Groundwork puts serving the highest above maintaining the status quo and personal comfort, and orients us towards what is most alive and aligned. Consciously doing Groundwork before applying the Chaordic Design framework infuses what follows with extra clarity and power.

- I have found Dee Hock's phrase "locus of power" to be very helpful when identifying principles. It is more pointed than, "How will we make decisions?" It calls for transparency, clarity, and integrity in how power is dealt with, and thereby helps human systems be less vulnerable to what Hock calls "the Four Beasts that inevitably devour their keeper: Ego, Envy, Avarice, and Ambition."[14] If more accessible language is important, I recommend keeping the word "power," by saying, for example, "where power rests," or "how power is dealt with." And the same for Hock's emphasis on "distribution of rewards." Find principles that give clear and robust guidance for the locus of power and the distribution of rewards. ∧

Possible pitfalls

- Notice whether you are holding back from going where Chaordic Design takes you. There are many reasons to want to bail out. This way of working challenges the status quo, ruffles feathers, and is like breaking new ground on the frontier. Pioneering is dedicated and passionate work. It takes a willingness to bear the discomfort of risk, ambiguity, and uncertainty. It requires facing push-back, from other people, and from our inner doubts and demons. The larger the initiative, the larger this pitfall is likely

---

14 Reprinted with permission of the publisher. From *Birth of the Chaordic Age*, 1999 by Dee Hock, Berrett-Koehler Publishers, Inc., San Francisco, CA. All rights reserved. www.bkconnection.com, page 17.

to be. Knowing it is there helps undo its power. When there is a lot of flack, it can mean we are close to the target. ∞

- One way groups indirectly hold back is to starve the process of the resources it needs. While any reflection on purpose and principles is valuable, for the breakthroughs Chaordic Design offers there needs to be enough time and facilitation savvy to delve deeper than typical strategic planning or visioning sessions. There needs to be scope for conversations to chart new territory, and in most contexts, this calls for making it a key priority for staff, bringing in outside facilitators, and ideally both. ↻ ∞

- Do not get caught in the trap of believing that you must have high level support. One can start anywhere, working with Chaordic Design in the areas where one has authority and freedom to move. One can be in a regular meeting and raise questions informed by Chaordic Design without ever saying "Let's use Chaordic Design." While high level support makes everything easier, it is not required.

- It is a mistake to see the Chaordic process as a straight-line, sequential process. Typical Chaordic Design processes are iterative: purpose, principles, more on the purpose in light of the principles, more on the principles in light of the newly framed purpose, and so on, considering how each of the six steps may inform and alter the others.

- While it is important to delve deeply at each stage, it is also important not to get bogged down. This requires discernment, as the natural tendency is to want to move on too soon. ↺ From time to time, put the process aside for a while. Come back later and look at things with fresh eyes. Stay open to what is trying to emerge. Know that creating effective human systems means birthing something new. Getting stuck at the early stages can kill the initiative, and moving too fast is likely to simply recreate a different version of the status quo.

CHAORDIC DESIGN

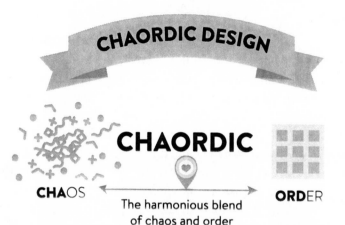

CHAORDIC

CHAOS ← The harmonious blend of chaos and order → **ORD**ER

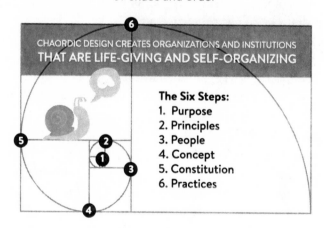

6

CHAORDIC DESIGN CREATES ORGANIZATIONS AND INSTITUTIONS
THAT ARE LIFE-GIVING AND SELF-ORGANIZING

The Six Steps:
1. Purpose
2. Principles
3. People
4. Concept
5. Constitution
6. Practices

DESIGN TO MITIGATE
THE FOUR BEASTS
THAT INEVITABLY DEVOUR THEIR KEEPER

EGO   ENVY   AVARICE   AMBITION

A way of life

When I was a teenager, I remember making the distinction between being *efficient* and being *effective*. I could see, for example, that I was efficient at passing exams but not effective in how I was using my time: I gained little in the way of meaningful knowledge or skills.

This disconnect – between what we are busy with and what really needs doing – is pandemic in our society. We are like Nasrudin of Sufi teaching stories, searching for lost keys under the streetlamp, rather than going into the shadows where he knows he dropped the keys. We choose the familiar path or the easier path, regardless of its relative futility, rather than the more demanding path where we can be truly effective.

It is important to be compassionate. There are good reasons for choosing the familiar. It is also important to stretch ourselves to act chaordically. Never in human history has it been more important for us to be effective at what is truly generative and lifegiving.

At the personal level

I invite you to close your eyes and take a few moments to reflect: Am I on purpose in my life? Where am I putting my time, energy, and attention? Is it aligned with what has most (or deepest) meaning for me, and with what brings me vibrantly alive? Am I making a contribution that I truly value and that I know is beneficial to others or to my context?[15]

For most of us, only a small portion of our time, energy, and attention goes to what is meaningful. I have been working chaordically for decades and still feel there is a gap between what I am doing and what I feel called to do. While Chaordic Design has helped me close the gap, it also keeps raising the bar!

In my experience, people often discount their purpose/calling, as it seems to come too naturally, joyously, and easily to count as a meaningful contribution.

---

15 In my experience as a coach, I find some people relate to the concept of "calling" or "life purpose" while others do not. If you are lucky enough to feel called, ask yourself, "Am I being true to my calling?"

Others do not relate at all to the concept of life purpose. There is so much pressure to adopt society's definition of what is important and worth pursuing, and to build lives focused on fitting in, making money, or being successful, substituting ersatz meaning for soul purpose. Others may have had clarity of purpose as a child or young person that was not welcomed in their social context, and so shut down on their passions in order to fit in. C

Chaordic Design asks big questions. It also gives big gifts: joy, wellbeing, fulfillment, peace of mind, and more. The people who choose to live consciously on purpose so enjoy the benefits that they rarely give up this way of orienting to life.

May all of us live ever and always with the questions: What is my purpose? Why am I here?

At the personal level, part two

Beyond these big picture questions, there are many other ways we can apply Chaordic Design at the personal level. It can be extremely helpful for clarifying how to approach a difficult conversation or parenting issue, or tackle a specific task.

In all cases, start by clarifying the purpose. What is at the core of what you aim to do? Be patient and rigorous in answering these questions. You will save yourself many false starts and much misplaced energy.

If you also take the time to articulate principles related to your purpose, you will have a much more robust touchstone for whatever is the focus of your design.

I cannot recommend too highly taking time to apply Chaordic Design to a current issue or challenge in your personal life. This framework takes second place in this book because it is so fundamental for effectiveness. Use it regularly and often so it becomes as natural and effortless as brushing your teeth.

Links to other chapters

Chaordic Design primarily links to other chapters through its focus on clarifying purpose and principles. Since clarity of purpose supports effectiveness, Chaordic Design is an excellent complement to every other framework. For example, if you realize you are stuck in a trap of rigidity or poverty, (Adaptive Cycle), having a clearly defined purpose helps you face the need for change. Anchoring to that purpose also gives you a crucial reference point and a stable base as you make the needed changes.

Clarity of purpose also offers an excellent foundation for working with Theory U – a framework for what to do when the past is no longer a good enough guide going forward. After using Chaordic Design to clarify purpose, Theory U offers a three-phase process for "leading from the future seeking to emerge." These two frameworks combined make a potent power pack for navigating this time in human history.

Perhaps the strongest link between Chaordic Design and the next framework, Generative Dialogue, is that the latter offers an excellent process for clarifying a group's purpose. The insights in the Generative Dialogue framework will help you tap into collective wisdom and the highest potential of your situation. Whether as a specific dialogue, or as ongoing practices of reflecting on assumptions and opening to new ways of seeing, you and your group are more likely to stay on purpose if you have conversations that are "generative" as defined in the pages to come.

3
Generative Dialogue

Great conversations are the lifeblood of effective action.

In situation after situation, I see a need for conversations that access our collective intelligence and that tap us into the creative source. That is why I delight in the Generative Dialogue framework. By naming four distinct "fields" of conversation, it offers a simple and powerful way for groups to see their own process – both where they are, and where things could go.

I have sketched the framework for interested friends and colleagues dozens of times on napkins in cafés, and on flipcharts in group settings. What excites me most is the way this lens charts territory currently outside most people's day-to-day experience. In doing so, the framework encourages new and more transformative levels of conversation – just as knowing there is a beautiful mountain nearby inspires us to climb to new heights.

Beyond naming what is possible, the Generative Dialogue framework offers a roadmap for creating better conversations and group processes. It helps you to see group dynamics, and identifies how to help dialogue be more powerful and effective. If you want to cultivate strong teams, create deeper levels of shared meaning, or support breakthrough thinking, you may get great value from this framework.

Origins

Otto Scharmer developed the Generative Dialogue framework in the late 1990s at the Massachusetts Institute of Technology (MIT). There he collaborated with others, including William Isaacs, an MIT lecturer and consultant who had been exploring dialogue as "the art of thinking together" since the mid-1980s.

Scharmer's intention was to map the evolution of conversations. There are other group-stage models that predate his work, such as Bruce Tuckman's "Forming, Storming, Norming, and Performing." What is potent and unique about the Generative Dialogue lens is the underlying structure, as you will see in the next section.

Scharmer's investigations helped him to create the framework of Generative Dialogue. It also led him to emphasize the importance of "presencing" in his later and ongoing work on Theory U (Chapter 6). ʊ̇

Scharmer's work is a great example of how distilling our understanding into frameworks (something everyone does on some level) is a living process – one we can interact with and adapt as called for by our emerging understanding.

Generative Dialogue

The Generative Dialogue framework is a classic four-quadrant model, created by drawing two lines which intersect at right angles. See if the description below of the terrain it maps matches your own experience in groups, perhaps by focusing on a current group context where you welcome fresh insight.

Group interactions typically start in the lower left quadrant. This first field of conversation is Politeness. At the outset of a conversation/meeting, people tend to be polite, paying more attention to social conventions than to their personal thoughts, feelings, and desires. ∧ We tend to say things we have said before, "downloading" stories, ideas, and opinions. This polite, rule-following behaviour reflects a "primacy of the whole" (for example, social conventions) and rote or non-reflective awareness, as defined by the two axes of the chart.

The Four Conversational Fields of Dialogue

Self-Reflective

IV.	III.
Flow Generative Dialogue	*Inquiry* Reflective Dialogue
- Presencing - Boundaries relax - Generative Listening (from future self and what wants to emerge) - Distributed sense of self within group (self as both self and group) - Commitment to emergence - Collective Intelligence & Synchronicity - Rule-generating - Creativity in the container	- Culture of Inquiry - Suspension of judgment & view - Tacit assumptions exposed - I am not my point of view - Empathic Listening - I-It to I-Thou relationship - I-I perspective - Slowing down - Rule-reflecting - Inquiry in the container

Primacy of   **Primacy of**
the   **the**
Whole   **Parts**

- Conformity or worse, collusion - Politeness & Caution (not saying what we are thinking/feeling) - Downloading mental models (ignore what is beneath surface) - Judgmental Listening (projection based on memory) - Rule-enacting (based on past) - Risks collusion & avoidance of undiscussables - Instability of container	- Argument culture - Expressiveness (saying what we think and feel) - Reactive (prone to polarization & move—oppose cycle) - Combative Listening (reloading) - Rule-revealing - Identified with own perspective as truth - Instability in the container
I.	II.
Politeness (Shared) Monologues	*Breakdown* Debate & Argument

Blaming &
Non-Reflective

Source: The titles of the axes and quadrants are used with permission from Otto Scharmer. The bullet points in the quadrants were developed by Kate Sutherland and Olen Gunnlaugson, and benefitted from the excellent and nuanced description of Scharmer's framework in *Dialogue and the Art of Thinking Together* by William Isaacs (see Further Resources).

The second field of conversation is Breakdown. Here, one or more people break social convention to say what they really think or feel. This rocks the "politeness" boat, sometimes triggering others to speak, or at least be in touch with their authentic thoughts and feelings. A single person breaks the ice and the group is now cracked into "primacy of the part."

The third field of conversation is Reflective Dialogue or Inquiry. For a group to get here, at least one person begins to reflect on their thoughts and positions. People "suspend" their thoughts and loosen their grip on previously unquestioned beliefs (e.g. maybe profit is not the only goal). This opens space for new ways of seeing and being.

The fourth field is Generative Dialogue, or Flow. It is the rarest field of conversation – a kind of peak experience where boundaries blur and people "think together." The conversation slows down. People listen deeply and silences are pregnant with shared meaning. It is common for people to complete each other's sentences. There is a palpable sense of oneness, as though whoever speaks voices the collective intelligence of the group. ↺

Navigating the quadrants

With the complex and pressing issues facing us at this time on our planet, we need to know how to shift groups into the two upper quadrants. In other words, now that we have a map showing us Inquiry and Flow, how do we get there?

Here is some of what the Generative Dialogue framework has to say about transitions between different fields of conversation:[1]

- Given time and a strong enough container, most groups naturally shift from Politeness to Breakdown. If groups stay in Politeness, it indicates that there is not much safety in the group. People might be afraid of humiliation, or some form of retribution. In other words, uncomfortable as it can be, Breakdown is a good sign.

---

1 For more of the rich insights available through this framework, please see *Dialogue and the Art of Thinking Together* by William Issacs.

- Often after breaking through to Breakdown, groups soon retreat to Politeness. The conversation is too "hot" and there is an exodus back to the comforts and predictability of social convention.

- It is also not unusual for groups to oscillate back and forth between the first two fields of conversation as frustration with the constraints of Politeness erupts into Breakdown, and discomfort with the heat of Breakdown sends people back to the familiar comforts of Politeness.

- For a group to move from Politeness to Breakdown, there needs to be enough stability in the container to take the heat. Groups sense intuitively if there is enough cohesion and connection to take the conversation to a deeper level. A cocktail party is emblematic of superficial politeness precisely because there is so much instability and self-consciousness in the configurations of people talking to each other.

- Groups cannot jump to Inquiry or Flow. An individual group member might be in a flow state, even at the outset of the conversation, but the group process tends to start in Politeness, and to get to Inquiry only by way of Breakdown.

- The shift from Breakdown to Inquiry begins when at least one person starts to question or otherwise get beyond their own assumptions and ways of thinking or perceiving. Scharmer recommends observing "with an open mind by suspending your voice of judgment." Rather than trying to get rid of judgment (arguably an impossible task), a powerful way forward is to inquire into our judgments and assumptions. "Is that true? What is another way to see this situation?" "What if the opposite were true?" One person authentically questioning in this way has the potential to shift the whole group into the conversation field of Inquiry.

- Inquiry is a radically different field of conversation from Politeness and Breakdown. The two lower quadrants are non-reflective: people are thinking in rule-following and habitual ways. When we access the capacity to witness our thoughts – when there is a bit of distance between what we are thinking and our sense of self as a thinker – then we are freed up to think in different ways. Shifting to the upper two quadrants supports breakthroughs and innovation.

- Having enough time is a necessary but not sufficient condition for reaching the upper quadrants. Conversations become richer when people's different perspectives stimulate new connections in the hearts and minds of others. Dialogue ripens when groups set aside two or three hours to delve deeply into a question or challenge. Most groups and organizations do not allow long enough stretches of time for a group to shift to the upper quadrants.

- The length of a session is a crucial element of what Scharmer calls "the container." Other elements are things like:

  o the quality of space (natural light, height of ceiling, quality of the air, sitting in a circle)

  o the quality of consciousness of the convenor/facilitator (open-mindedness, open-heartedness, non-judgmental, curious), O ♺ and

  o the purpose for the conversation – is there a clear focus? Framing things as an evocative question tends to both focus the conversation and elicit different ways of thinking. If the conversation is framed as, "We need to make a decision about X issue," that tends to produce problem-solving ways of thinking rather than Inquiry or Flow. ⌒

- The shift from Inquiry to Flow comes as group members place their attention on discovering the future seeking to unfold. ♺ Scharmer calls this "presencing," by which he means both being present in this moment, and bringing into the moment the future that is seeking to emerge. People listen deeply – paying attention to what others are saying, to the energy in the group, and to whatever else catches their attention. ∧ These are meaningful signals, pointing to the

GENERATIVE DIALOGUE

SELF-REFLECTIVE

SHARED MEANING
EMERGENCE &

I WONDER WHY I SEE IT THIS WAY?

JUDGMENTS

ASSUMPTIONS

BELIEFS

PART

3. INQUIRY

I DISAGREE!

2. BREAKDOWN

4. FLOW

DO I REALLY NEED TO BE HERE FOR THIS CONVERSATION?

WHOLE

1. POLITENESS

BLAH BLAH
BLAH BLAH

MONOLOGUE

BLAMING / NOT SELF-REFLECTIVE

DEEP LIFE-GIVING CONVERSATIONS THIS WAY

HOW CAN WE THINK TOGETHER?

emerging future. As with Politeness, there is primacy of the whole. Flow is a field of conversation where the group is like a satellite dish, picking up and amplifying signals that are guiding us forward.

What does Generative Dialogue look like in practice? Sometimes it is a facilitated dialogue session on a specified topic. At other times, Generative Dialogue becomes part of the culture of a workplace. Both are valid and important. See the story below for a great illustration of how Generative Dialogue supports breakthroughs in thinking, in part by opening up our sense of identity.

Generative Dialogue in action

Marika Sandrelli admits she signed up for a course on Generative Dialogue to raise her status at work. At the time, she was a Project Coordinator on contract to a Health Authority to oversee projects for people with addictions. She was also one of the few in her work context without professional certification, and she wanted high-powered words and concepts to drop into memos and policy conversations.

Instead, the first session rocked her world. She understood at a deep level that rather than accumulating information and sophisticated language, there was more vitality and possibility when she suspended assumptions, and was willing to feel the awkwardness of not knowing.

The shattering of her illusions hurt, but there was no going back. She could no longer put energy into accumulating information and gaining credibility in the eyes of others. This threw her into an identity crisis. She saw that the mental health and substance abuse system she worked in was "dismembering" – slicing and dicing people and the issues they were working with. Such analysis distanced the employees; it was a way to keep safely above it all, and even a form of social control.

As she came through the crisis, Marika "remembered" a sense of self that was rooted in her core values of expressing creativity and love. She soon discovered others keen for dialogue that went beyond conventional thinking about addictions and substance abuse.

As a specific example, Marika and her colleagues had conversations about stigma – the shame, disgrace, or humiliation often felt by people with mental health and/or substance use issues. Stigma is a huge barrier to effective treatment, and is traditionally seen as something to reduce or outwit.

Reflecting more deeply, Marika and her colleagues realized that they had been seeing stigma as a standardized variable, like income level – some commodified "thing" that a person has more or less of.

They began to explore what lay behind stigma, and quickly found what Marika called "a land of possibilities." Instead of stigma being a barrier and a variable, she and her colleagues came to see stigma as a doorway into rich and life-changing conversations about beliefs, perceptions, and histories.

Though not comfortable, staff began to examine how they were showing up to sessions with their clients, and how they were inadvertently contributing to the stigma felt by clients. "A world has opened up," Marika said. "The collective emotional intelligence has increased exponentially."

Marika cites extensive research showing that treatment for substance use is most effective when staff are able to establish good rapport early in the process. The conversations about stigma have helped staff be kinder, and more able to "join the client" on their journey. The resulting greater connectedness is reducing "no shows" and improving outcomes.

I love how Marika's story illustrates the interconnections between the personal and professional aspects of her life. While she was interested in learning about Generative Dialogue primarily for professional development, exposure to the framework challenged her very identity, and her core ways of thinking. In turn, this has given her keys to open "doors of possibility", profoundly transforming the conversations and outcomes in her work. The ripples continue!

At the personal level

I hope you will follow Marika's example and apply Generative Dialogue in your own life.[2] To build your "muscles" for living more generatively:

- Ask "What core beliefs and assumptions run me (either in general, or in a specific context)? This is a bit challenging, so it can be helpful to have a conversation with a buddy. Together you can bring warm curious attention to each other's "articles of faith", the building blocks of how you each understand the world/your situation. Potent entry points include:

  o How I define success;
  o My theories of how change happens;
  o My attitudes toward conflict;
  o My sense of self worth;
  o My ideas about the future.

  Once you have identified an assumption or core belief, you can ask yourself "Is it true?" and what it would mean for how I live if the opposite were true. In this process, you will be able to see that often your core beliefs are simply thoughts you have adopted wholesale, many of them conditioned by your upbringing. C

- Suspend judgments. This starts with noticing what you define as good or right, and what you label bad or wrong. Suspending judgments does not mean we have to abandon discernment. Rather it invites us to slow down enough to inquire into that which we normally speed over. Our judgments keep us from seeing and hearing more fully, from meeting one another. For example we might judge a colleague to be a self-important bigot, and so lose the kernels of wisdom in a perspective that is radically different from our own. As said by the great mystic poet Rumi, "Out beyond ideas of wrongdoing and rightdoing, there is a field. I'll meet you there."

---

2   This is a never-ending journey, and wonderful support to the work on yourself as an instrument of change as explored in the Groundwork chapter.

- Listen generatively. Building on the previous bullet point, there is a way of listening that is radically open. Think of the difference between a spotlight – with its narrow targeted beam – and a floodlight – with its wider and more diffuse focus. To internalize this distinction, take a moment now to look at something 8-10 feet away from you. Then, without moving your head, soften your gaze to take in everything else in your field of vision. When we focus like a spotlight, we are generally looking to confirm our current beliefs and ways of being. When we focus like a floodlight, we are more open to seeing ourselves and our world differently, and we are also more open to what Scharmer calls, "the future seeking to emerge." With practice, you will be able to shift back and forth with ease between these two ways of seeing/being/listening.

Here are other ways you can apply Generative Dialogue at the personal level. Can you join with others to reframe a barrier or challenge as a doorway? What resistance or irritation might you become curious about? What word or phrase in daily use can you put under the microscope to tease out hidden assumptions and limiting beliefs?

While these reflections take time, and often involve the discomfort of shedding the "know a lot" identity, you are likely to find that there is no going back. Being on the edge of new worlds of possibility is too compelling, and the greater engagement is so wonderfully alive.

It would be wonderful if, from time to time, we would all practice slowing things down so we could, paradoxically, achieve better outcomes more quickly and with more grace and ease.

Here are finer points and possible pitfalls to consider should you go forward with this framework.

Finer points

- Sometimes there is a mismatch between the purpose of the meeting and Generative Dialogue as a particular form of conversation. For example, do not use Generative Dialogue when the situation requires a focused problem-solving session to tackle a particular operational issue. That said, to achieve breakthroughs on the many challenging specific issues we face, dialogue has important gifts to offer. Systems Theory[3] tells us that the "fixes" for many of our specific challenges actually create more problems. We need to think together, and to think differently, now more than ever.

- When convening a conversation, be mindful of how you frame the topic. Ideally, the focus is vivid, interesting, and compelling. You might frame the issue as an appreciative question that expresses your core purpose: + "How can we have food on every table?" You might create a provocative proposition: "Denial of death is the root of our healthcare crisis." Often the planning conversation about how to frame the focus needs as much or more time as the dialogue itself. ☉

Possible pitfalls

- A common pitfall is not valuing Politeness. All four fields of conversation are important, the way infancy, childhood, adolescence, and adulthood are each wonderful and necessary parts of the human journey. These days, it is a significant accomplishment simply to get everyone together in one room. The least generative field of conversation, Politeness, needs to be valued because without it, we cannot get to other fields of conversation. Politeness is like a courting dance – a ritualized way we begin the process of weaving connections and possibility. It helps create the container for all that follows.

- Manipulation is another common pitfall. There can be a temptation to "get things moving" by, for example, expressing

---

3   See the first item, Systems Theory, in Further Resources.

strong opinions or feelings in the hopes that this instigates Breakdown. When we speak strongly as an authentic expression of what is going on for us, we serve the group. When we speak strongly with a manipulative intention, we damage trust. We might provoke Breakdown, but it will have a different, more forced flavour. The most powerful way to support group unfoldment is to be authentic. This means being as present as we can to what is unfolding within and through us, and not taking on the role of "making something happen." ↻

- Expectations set back group process. One example of this is expecting my group to achieve Inquiry in this meeting because we reached Inquiry in our last meeting. It is like expecting great sex every time: the pressure is counterproductive. At the same time, knowing that Inquiry and Flow are possible is helpful. An elder once advised me: "Have expectancy, not expectations."

- The richness and delights of Flow can lead to the setback of wanting to remain in the Flow state. Scharmer speaks of the "crisis of re-entry": to implement the insights and shared meaning gained in Flow, we must re-enter the world and return to the conversation fields of Politeness and Breakdown. Like meditators, we need to come down from the mountain and take action in the marketplace.

- Sometimes people fail to value the full richness of Inquiry and Flow. We assume that what is said equals what happened – that meeting minutes accurately reflect the accomplishments of the meeting. What is spoken is only the visible tip of a much bigger iceberg that is below the surface. Nine-tenths of what unfolds is in the invisible interiors – in the hearts and minds of people present. Invisible as they are, it is important to value the changes of heart and perspective, the growth of shared meaning, and the emergence of collective intelligence.

- Do not assume that because the group as a whole is in a specific field of conversation that everyone in the group is at that level. ∧ An individual can be in Flow while the rest of the group is in Politeness. You do not need to do anything about this. If you notice you are withholding what you have to offer, this simple awareness may be enough to help you let go of any need to be understood. Share your thoughts briefly, and as if people understood you perfectly.

If the above points raise questions for you, great! Give yourself the gift of following up on recommendations in the Generative Dialogue section in Further Resources. I particularly recommend William Isaac's book, *Dialogue and the Art of Thinking Together*. It was my introduction to Scharmer's Generative Dialogue framework, and is chockablock full of insights, practical pointers, and inspiring stories.

Links to other chapters

Generative Dialogue applies to every framework that involves groups of humans being and thinking together (all of them).

You do not need to formally introduce the Generative Dialogue framework or work with it explicitly. When you make it a practice to question your assumptions, to open to different ways of thinking, and to listen for the future seeking to emerge, you cannot help but spark more generative conversations and group processes.

Bringing attention and inquiry to what is already working well (Appreciative Inquiry) is great fodder for a generative conversation. So is creating a high trust environment (Groundwork) where people are more likely to open up – both to what matters most for them, and to new ways of seeing and being.

The Flow field of conversation is particularly linked to Conscious Co-creation and Theory U. When groups of people are reflective and "co-presencing,"[4] there is a sense of being tapped into the current of life. Conscious Co-creation and Theory U point to that same connection to life.

The next chapter introduces the Adaptive Cycle framework – a way of seeing how human and natural systems unfold over the long term. The Adaptive Cycle calls us to reflect on the big picture

---

4   We will get to what "co-presencing" means in the Theory U chapter.

of where we have come from, where we are now, and where we are going – an excellent opportunity for Generative Dialogue.

It takes courage to have reflective conversations. They are so powerful for getting us unstuck and moving toward what is more alive. May the next chapter help you to be resilient over the long-term.

Questions

Here are some questions you can ask yourself during any conversation.

- What field of conversation are we in?

- How open is my mind and heart? Am I grounded, centered, and fully present? Am I able to suspend assumptions, judgments, and beliefs?

- What future is trying to emerge? What am I noticing? Am I open to it?

- Can I appreciate everything about the group conversation, exactly as it is, while holding space for the conversation to deepen and go to unprecedented places?

- What can I do to create the highest quality container for my group conversation? How engaging and generative is the invitation/topic? How can I improve the quality of our meeting space?

4
Adaptive Cycle

Change feels like death, but it is sure death not to change.

I first heard of C.S. (Buzz) Holling's work in 2001 when people in community development circles were talking about resilience. It sounded up my alley – cutting edge and interesting – but I did not take the time to follow up. Then curiosity about social innovation led me to a book[1] where his Adaptive Cycle was an organizing framework, and I was smitten.

Holling's framework sheds light on how human systems change over time. It offers the long view – a very important perspective in our current crisis/short-term fixated world – and helps us see how life moves through cycles of creation and destruction. I particularly appreciate that it busts the linear growth "world as machine" paradigm that has been dominant for the past two hundred years.

The Adaptive Cycle framework calls us to have courageous conversations. By offering a simple, powerful, and big picture way to name what is, it helps group members get on the same page, and opens space for facing tough issues and making bold choices. Like many, I want to deny the need for such "tough love." Holling's

---

1   I highly recommend *Getting to Maybe: How the World is Changed* by Frances Westley, Brenda Zimmerman and Michael Quinn Patton. See Further Resources.

framework shows the cost of denial and avoidance, and encourages us to embrace change, to value small-scale experimentation, and to be ready to seize opportunities. ↺

Facing the collapse of our financial, medical, judicial, and other social systems, compounded by climate change and our ever-tighter interconnectedness, the Adaptive Cycle is more relevant than ever. To navigate these unprecedented waters, we need its keen insights, its faith in life, and its spirit of adventure.

Origins

The inspiration for the Adaptive Cycle came from nature. ↺ Starting in the 1950s, Holling, an ecological scientist, had a passion to understand population processes. He asked, "What are the relationships between predator and prey?" In the course of his research, he developed models that were "simple, but not too simple,"[2] that explained population processes for insects, birds, fish, and even submarines!

With the advent of computers, Holling developed simulations, and in the process discovered multi-stable states: "population systems were not driven only by attraction to a single equilibrium state but, instead, there were several equilibrium states that determined their existence."[3]

Holling learned from nature to look for the interplay of slow and quick variables. His study of forest ecology, for example, taught him that common "decades-long fire protection policies" (slow) by forest managers have contributed to widespread demise of forests due, among other factors, to outbreaks of insects (quick).

In other words, where humans have interfered with nature, nature's rules have ultimately reasserted themselves, often in ways that are catastrophic for all concerned.

---

2   Gunderson, Lance and C. S. Holling. *Panarchy: Understanding Transformations in Human and Natural Systems.* Washington, DC: Island Press, 2001, page 409.

3   Holling, C.S. 2011. *Global Resilience Requires Novelty: A Speech by Buzz Holling.* http://aidontheedge.info/2011/10/25/global-resilience-requires-novelty-a-speech-by-buzz-holling/

It turns out that Holling's work, so firmly rooted in ecological science, also has important light to shed on human systems.

Adaptive Cycle

The Adaptive Cycle is a theoretical framework focused on "the interplay between change and persistence, between the predictable and unpredictable."[4] The intention is to offer practical guidance for complex situations, such as where economic, ecological, and institutional systems interact.

The goal of the Adaptive Cycle is "resilience." Here is the definition from the book that first ignited my interest in this framework:

> Resilience is the capacity to experience massive change and yet still maintain the integrity of the original. Resilience isn't about balancing change and stability. It isn't about reaching an equilibrium state. Rather, it is about how massive change and stability paradoxically work together.[5]

From studying what supports long-term resilience in forests and other ecosystems, Holling identified the Adaptive Cycle. Shown graphically, a system that is resilient loops continuously through the following four stages:

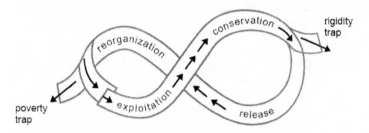

Release: A disaster or crisis, such as a (naturally occurring) forest fire, destroys existing structures. While generally lamented, the destruction releases resources for new growth.

---

4   Gunderson and Holling, ibid., page 5.

5   Westley, et al., page 65

Reorganization: A time of exciting new opportunities and new connections. There is intense competition for resources as new strategies jockey for position.

Exploitation: The system picks a small number of winning options, and invests heavily in them.

Conservation: The system matures. Structures are developed and become dominant. There is little room and few resources for new ideas or ways of doing things.

It follows that lack of resilience (and system dis-ease) comes from getting stuck, illustrated here as getting caught in either:

- *The Poverty Trap:* resources are spread too thin or none of the new ideas take root enough to move to the next phase, **or**

- *The Rigidity Trap:* The system fails to release resources for new growth (innovation!) and rigidifies.

What light does this framework shed on your own life and group, or on the issues making headlines in your community? In recent years, this framework has been plumbed for insights into all sorts of contexts, including small businesses, social programs, and local economies.

What if budget cutbacks are like Holling's forest fires? What if our medical, judicial, and educational systems are trapped in rigidity? These and other questions point to embracing change (innovation) as a crucial element in resilient/healthy systems!

Here is a story from Doug Cohen, a wise and patient cultivator of leadership for greater resilience and sustainability who consults and volunteers all over the Western Hemisphere. He first heard of Holling's work in 2004, and it complemented his prior understanding of Systems Theory. In all his work with change agents and human systems, Cohen brings the long view, and he is mindful, for example, of how periods of relative stability mask micro changes that are building towards the next release phase.

ADAPTIVE CYCLE

What will help us be resilient over time?
How can massive change and stability paradoxically work together?

RIGIDITY TRAP

CRISIS

MATURITY

RELEASE

EXPLORATION

DEVELOPMENT

POVERTY TRAP

CHOICE

★ IMPORTANT TO ASK ★

WHERE ARE WE?

Adaptive Cycle in action

Within days of Haiti being devastated by the major earthquakes in January 2010, I began a conversation with my colleague, Jonathan Cloud, about opportunities to support greater resilience and sustainability in that country.

At the time, he and I were both part of the Institute for Sustainable Enterprise (ISE) at Fairleigh Dickinson University. Our work to articulate an ISE approach to contributing in Haiti received a further boost when Jonathan was approached by a gentleman from the U.S. Department of Homeland Security who knew there would be tremendous need due to the earthquake and because he believed our institute could be helpful in ways that his department could not.

Galvanized by this Federal government interest, ISE created a White Paper, and the response to that paper made it possible for Jonathan and me to travel to Miami for the first Sustainable Haiti Conference in March 2010. That was a scouting trip to ask the question, "How can we help?"

We had already seen the vast outpouring of financial support from individuals and governments around the world, and the almost total lack of mechanisms on the ground in Haiti to distribute resources.

Knowing that the earthquakes had precipitated a massive release phase in Haitian society, we already knew that a key contribution would be taking the long view going forward. Right from the outset, we framed the conversation as co-creating a 100-year vision of a resilient Haiti.

From our work in other contexts, we also knew that within the complexity of the Haitian situation, parallel to the relative ineffectiveness of the world bodies' attempts to make solutions, there were resilient human response systems with still-to-be-tapped workable solutions for Haiti's problems.

As a result, on the very first day at the Sustainable Haiti Conference, we conceived of and launched the Sustainable Haiti Coalition, and began to sign people up. The Coalition was designed as an ecosystem that could receive and nurture the seeds of the reorganization phase. More specifically, it was a platform for people to meet and generate productive proposals with each other.

While signing people up, we invited them to the first gathering of the Coalition, which we held on the third day of the conference. There we opened a space for dialogue on workable solutions. We were cultivating connections, trust, and community to greatly increase opportunities for what I call 'Velcro moments' – the times when there is a good solid fit between what certain people offer and what others either add in to it, or draw from it.

Emerging out of that first session, we created a few simple structures to support ongoing networking and collaboration. The main one is a monthly conference call/webinar where members of the Coalition can present proposals, and others can either join them in the initiative in some way or become beneficiaries. Another is the ongoing networking and linking that Jonathan and I do, nurturing initiatives one-on-one.

Through patience and stick-to-itiveness, we have learned better ways to support collaborations as we have gone along. For example, we are much more proactive in building relationships, trust, and momentum (buzz) leading up to the annual Sustainable Haiti Conference, and at the conference too, prior to our Coalition session, which is always scheduled for the third and final day.

As a result, the offers got stronger and the collaborations richer. For instance, in 2012, one person put out an offer to create a specific solution for future education programs. Others, inspired by the possibilities, offered personal connections and financial support to expedite and amplify the initiative.

There were many other productive collaborations too, such as for food and sustainable agriculture, sanitation, micro-finance, energy efficiency, renewable energy, and more.

Many of the solutions are what I call "dual social benefit." For example, one member of the Coalition was an avid mountain biker passionate about the potential to garner support from the international mountain biking community for "voluntourism" to build a system of bike trails in the spectacularly beautiful Haitian countryside. With support from the Coalition, a feasibility study was undertaken for a project that has the economic benefit of increased tourism (short-term and long-term) as mountain bikers visit Haiti to build, and then ride on, special trails, and the economic development from bicycle-related and other businesses to service those people and the project.

In terms of the Adaptive Cycle, I know that there need to be many experiments to pioneer workable solutions for Haiti going forward. The Sustainable Haiti Coalition is one coordinating mechanism among hundreds for helping in Haiti. What keeps me going is that we get real traction on issues. Creating a platform for a diverse group of people to connect and form collaborations works. Yes it takes time, but the solutions people come up with move forward steadily, and they are often beneficial both to satisfy immediate needs and for cultivating greater resilience over the long term.

Cohen's story is a big picture application of the Adaptive Cycle, one that informs his practice in favour of the long view and supports diverse experiments in reorganization phases. I hope you can see why the Adaptive Cycle is a core framework in many social innovation capacity-building programs.

Working with the Adaptive Cycle

You can use the Adaptive Cycle framework as a diagnostic for any human system. It can help you to articulate what you already know about your group, or point to gaps in your knowledge. Either way, you can gain insight into your context by asking what phase it is in, and whether it is in one of the traps.

You will likely soon see that your situation is layered. Different adaptive cycles may unfold at different scales, depending on niche, local, regional, or national influences. Your department, for example, might be in a Conservation phase, within a broader organizational context that is in a Reorganization phase. These in turn may unfold within sector dynamics and the many adaptive cycles of government policy and the regional, national, and global economies. The basic dynamic of the four-stage Adaptive Cycle applies at each scale, AND there can be interesting "cross-scale" interactions, such as where innovation at one scale precipitates release at another (see Finer Points).

Another option is to invite others – such as members of an organization, company, or sector – to apply the framework to their own context. This kind of stocktaking can be very beneficial at planning sessions or annual retreats. Most people grasp the model quickly when walked through a diagram of the four phases. You can introduce the framework and then have people talk in pairs about how it applies to their situation. You can also have a group dialogue ⟲ to surface different perspectives. In all cases, encourage group members to appreciate the two core messages of the framework: getting caught in traps is commonplace, and resilience comes from constantly moving through the adaptive cycle.

◆◆◆

The following points tease out more aspects of the Adaptive Cycle framework. See whether the added dimensions are helpful to you. Embrace those that serve your purpose, and leave the rest. Find the level that is complex enough, but not too complex.

Finer points

- The Adaptive Cycle framework distinguishes between the front loop of the adaptive cycle and the back loop. The front loop is the more familiar process of exploitation and conservation – where a few options emerge as winners and the system focuses on maximizing efficiency and growth. Change, while constant, is routine. The refinement and growth of a new manufactured product is a classic front loop example. The back loop profiles the more chaotic process of release and reorganization. Change is either catastrophic or transformational. The current massive shift from paper to digital formats in media and publishing provides one example.

- The adaptive cycle graphic on page 73 may give the misleading impression that the phases are roughly equal in length. Systems typically have longer front loop phases, and more abrupt and rapid back loop phases.

- The back loop offers significant opportunities for shaping what goes forward in the next front-loop cycle. ↺ A single individual or small group has much greater influence on the overall system through piloting new approaches and creating new connections, right when the previously dominant regime is breaking down and releasing resources. One needs to be nimble, and only a fraction of the new ideas will go forward. Rather than trying to patch up the old regime, it is important to embrace change, link with others to accelerate learning, and to create rapid prototypes. ↺

- The Adaptive Cycle distinguishes two main "cross-scale" interactions: revolt and remembrance.

  Relatively rare, revolt is where changes in a smaller-scale adaptive cycle trigger the release phase in a larger, slower adaptive cycle. For example, when the timing was right, a few people with hammers precipitated the collapse of the Berlin Wall. ∧

  In a Remembrance interaction, resources stored in a large, slow cycle influence a smaller, quicker cycle to reorganize in ways that "remember" the larger, slower cycle. An example of this are seeds that lie dormant until activated by a forest fire, and support previously present species to reappear.

- Implicit in the framework is deep respect for natural cycles, including a fundamental optimism that even if human interventions long prop up unhealthy situations, ultimately the inherent creativity and diversity of life will emerge.

- Holling identifies our current global situation as the third or fourth major "pulse" or period of transformation[6] in human history. As we face potentially immense and unpredictable destruction and reorganization, his overarching recommendation is to

---

6   Previous pulses include the agricultural revolution, the industrial revolution, and now the "global interconnected communications-driven revolution."

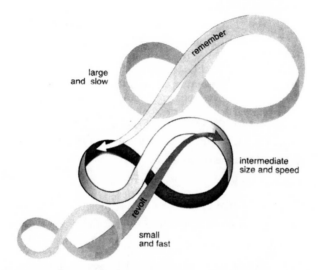

large
and slow

intermediate
size and speed

small
and fast

Source: *Panarchy* edited by Lance H. Gunderson and C.S. Holling. Copyright 2002, Island Press. Reproduced by permission of Island Press, Washington, D.C.

Haiti update – 'Remembrance' in action

Sadly, another example of Remembrance is what unfolded for the Sustainable Haiti Coalition mentioned in the Adaptive Cycle in action section.

In the five years since my 2012 conversations with Cohen, the Coalition was not able to sustain momentum for resilience over the long-term. Once the headlines and world attention moved away from Haiti, it was not long until funding was cut for the Coalition's work. Jonathan Cloud held on as long as he could, but finally archived the website and shifted his attention to other places where he could get more traction.

Deep transformation has yet to happen in Haiti. Despite this sobering update, the long-view strategies derived from the Adaptive Cycle remain valid for Haiti. The Adaptive Cycle also helps us understand how deep, longstanding patterns of leaving Haiti to its own devices were soon "remembered" as cycles dominant in the wider landscape reasserted themselves.

Source: Email communication from Jonathan Cloud.

experiment. He advocates "a host of safe-fail experiments[7] to test new ways of communicating, living, and sustaining our foundations." Here are Holling's specific suggestions:[8]

1. Encourage innovation through a rich variety of experiments and transformative approaches that probe possible directions. It is important to encourage experiments that have a low cost of failure to individuals, the environment, and careers, because many of these will fail. △

2. Reduce inhibitions to change, which are common when systems get locked up.

3. Protect and communicate the accumulated knowledge and experience needed for change.

4. Promote discourse among all parties involved to try to foster curiosity, courage, and clarity about change. ↺

5. Encourage new foundations for renewal that build and sustain the ability of people, economies, and nature to deal with change, and ensure that these new foundations consolidate and expand our understanding of change.

6. Allow sufficient time. This pulse is a global phenomenon, and it could potentially affect all levels of the hierarchy, all the

The Long View in Haiti

There are organizations working to cultivate Haiti's resilience over the long term. Shining examples include Partners in Health, 100K Jobs for Haiti, and Hope for Haiti. These organizations predated the earthquake and have continued after it, and their focus is addressing the root causes of Haiti's social challenges – including access to good jobs and support for greater food self sufficiency.

Source: Email communication from Jonathan Cloud.

---

7 "Safe-fail" experiments are designed so there are no serious negative consequences if the experiments fail and any "failures" in the experiment shed important light on a complex system.

8 Holling, C.S. 2004. "From complex regions to complex worlds." Ecology and Society 9(1): 11. http://www.ecologyandsociety.org/vol9/iss1/art11/

way up the chain, from the individual/family to national and global systems.

Notice how Holling's suggestions could be in the Theory U chapter! I believe the same applies to the pitfalls below. ↻

Possible pitfalls

- While the framework helps us to see unfolding events as part of a wider, healthier process of resilience, this does not mean we should ignore or discount the suffering and distress people may be experiencing. It is important to have compassion for ourselves, and for people, communities, and entities that are in one of the traps or in the process of being "creatively destroyed."

- The discomfort and chaos of the back loop means that we typically want to move on as quickly as possible. Whether at the personal level or beyond, it is important to allow ourselves and our systems to let go fully rather than clinging to the old or trying to patch things together again. In such times, it is helpful do the three-step Groundwork practice as a way of connecting to the part of one's self that is enduring and always at peace, and to choose to trust, as outlined in the Groundwork chapter. ○ When fear is high because of change and uncertainty, it is important to find the part of ourselves that can join Jack Gibb in saying, "I know that no matter what happens, at some very deep level, I will be OK."[9]

- Not all resilience is healthy. Some highly toxic systems endure for excessively long periods of time. The regimes of Idi Amin, Pinochet, and Duvalier come to mind. A recent example is the lack of any real change in the regulation of western financial institutions after the burst of the sub-prime bubble in 2008. It is important to discern healthy from unhealthy resilience.

---

9   This quote thanks to Marilyn Waller. For more of her story about working with Gibb, see http://www.katersutherland.com/wp/wp-content/uploads/2017/07/Trust-Theory-Oc9.pdf

- Not all innovation is healthy. Frances Westley and others name what they see as "the paradox of innovation: innovation is both a contributing cause for our current unsustainable trajectory and our hope for tipping in new more resilient directions."[10] While it may not be easy to know the difference, it is important to avoid negative, unintended consequences from our well-intended innovative actions.[11]

At the personal level

Like all the frameworks in this book, the Adaptive Cycle also applies at the personal level. Here are suggestions and questions to help you access its potent and important insights. The bonus is that these same reflection prompts can be applied at other scales too.

The best place to start is by considering where you are in the four-phase adaptive cycle. You may notice that different elements of your life (career, marriage, relationships) are at different phases, and you would be in good company if part of your life is caught in a poverty or rigidity trap. Add to this consideration of the phases of people close to you and you can do a niche-scale reflection on cross-scale interactions. For example, if your child will leave the nest soon, what Release might that pitch you into?

You can also identify your "phase orientation" – the phase where there is a good fit with your strengths, temperament, and ways of working. If you are not already based where you shine, perhaps it is time for you to instigate a personal back loop!

Once you know where you are in the cycle(s) of your life, a great next question is how to cultivate your resilience. Here are some key considerations for each phase:

---

10 Source: Frances Westley et al., Tipping Toward Sustainability: Emerging Pathways of Transformation. *Ambio*, 2011 November; 40(7): 762–780.

11 While generally successful, the international mountain biking project in Haiti, mentioned in Cohen's story, has had some negative unintended consequences. The biking events actually happened in 2013 and 2014, but there was not a long-term commitment to this initiative, and as a result "voluntourism" has a bad name in Haiti. Source: Email from Jonathan Cloud.

Release: The primary task in this phase is sense-making. ↺ Release means you are in a time of massive change, perhaps including chaos and crisis. It can be very uncomfortable and disorienting, but it is also a potent opportunity to rethink your purpose and worldview. What is it time to let go of? Who in your networks can you connect with for reflective, creative, and inspiring conversations?

Journaling can be a helpful tool, or perhaps you prefer other ways to articulate, map, or list the different dimensions of your current situation. If you feel you are "too busy" for self-care in midst of the chaos, consider that it is precisely at these times that Groundwork ○ is most important! Being better connected to your center/essence will help you to be nimble and responsive, and to grow your trust in the process of unraveling, the better to be able to reshape yourself into something new!

Reorganization: The primary task in this phase is experimentation. Reorganization is a time of brainstorming options and exploring new possibilities. What helps you see things with fresh perspective? What nourishes your creativity? For many of us, it is helpful to discuss ideas with others who share our passion – and the more diverse that group is, the better. Perhaps there are books, or conferences, or websites where you can source inspiration at this time. And the Internet is your friend: it is a great way to research what others are doing and learn more about potential options.

To help you stay open to the uncertainty and ambiguity of experimenting, consider how to grow your tolerance for risk and false starts. Here, again, Groundwork is helpful. Perhaps there is someone you can partner with who has more comfort with the unknown, or who brings skillsets and experience you lack. △ Perhaps you can interweave different, already-proven ideas and initiatives in new ways – a tried and true strategy in many innovations.

Exploitation: Nimble, fast-paced development is the name of the game in this phase. The key question is: What will you focus on? In Reorganization, you were encouraged to consider your many options and to run lots of experiments. To avoid the Poverty Trap in this new phase, you need to have the courage to let go of most of your ideas so that you can focus on the one (or few) that are the most promising. With that decision made, it is as if you are in start-up mode, with dozens of tasks that need to be dealt with right away. It is important to consider your priorities on an ongoing basis, and to ask what is "good enough" so that you keep all the different elements moving forward.

Conservation: This longer, slower-paced phase is preoccupied with efficiency and productivity. In it, most of your energy goes into developing and improving systems and procedures. Growth creates opportunities for greater specialization, and more possibility for you to focus on what you do best. At the same time, resilience calls us to open up and challenge our ways of seeing, right in the midst of everything going well. What can you do to challenge your perspectives, worldview, and thought habits? You might go to a conference outside your immediate field, or follow a blog from another sector/industry. It is also important to scan the environment for changes in your context that might spell the end of your current way of doing things. For example, which emerging or current trends/technologies influence your options or choices? From time to time, it is also important to ask: Is it time for me to disrupt myself, and leave a job, or line of work, or a relationship?

◆◆◆

It can be challenging to take such an honest look at yourself. Doing so rocks the boat. Using the Adaptive Cycle framework calls us to constantly change and adapt as we move through its four phases. These personal reflections will help you have compassion as you hold out the mirror for others and groups to see themselves. It will also help you integrate working with the Adaptive Cycle, and to have ongoing access to its support for greater resiliency and innovation!

Links to other chapters

The Adaptive Cycle's long-view calls for courageous conversations about letting some things go and making tough choices between emerging options. Such conversations are best nurtured where there is trust (Groundwork), an appreciative lens (Appreciative Inquiry), and a strong sense of purpose (Chaordic Design).

Similarly, as we face the need for systems change and bold forays into the unknown, Theory U offers a helpful perspective and road map.

Process Oriented Psychology and Integral Theory call us to be mindful that at any one time different subgroups can be experiencing different phases of the adaptive cycle. For example, some regions of the globe are already dealing with massive economic and social disruption due to climate change, while other areas are much less affected.

Enterprise Facilitation is another lens with profound faith in the hidden potential in life. Enterprise Facilitation has helped transform some of the most economically depressed areas in the planet. If Holling and so many others are correct that we are on the brink of massive systems failure, then the perspective of Enterprise Facilitation has a great deal to offer. Check out the next chapter to see how a grassroots, highly replicable way of connecting a few key dots can spark wonderful new enterprises and community initiative.

Questions

- What phase of the adaptive cycle are we in?
- How will what we do in this phase influence following phases?
- Are we caught in a trap of poverty or rigidity?
- Do others in the system agree that this is the phase/trap we are in?
- How can we take care of each other as we move ourselves out of the trap of poverty/rigidity?
- What experiments can we undertake?
- What are potential negative consequences from any of our well-intended innovative actions?

5
Enterprise Facilitation

Alone we can do so little; together we can do so much.

Helen Keller

I remember devouring Ernesto Sirolli's book *Ripples from the Zambezi – Passion, Entrepreneurship and the Rebirth of the Local Economy*. Its many success stories helped me see possibilities for a large project I was working on at the time. It also identified a key role missing in community development efforts of all types. My word had been "broker" – someone to help make connections between different parts of a system. Sirolli called the role "enterprise facilitator" reflecting his focus on small-scale, for profit businesses.

I believe we do not adequately see or value the importance of networkers, connectors, linkers, and facilitators. Valuing this function, and backing it with resources, has huge potential to shift the needle on poverty, sustainability, and other big issues facing us.

This framework also shines the light on the three dimensions that most need linking. I think of it as an asset-based approach on steroids. Not only do we look for assets – we particularly focus on making connections between three distinct types of assets. Therein lies the magic of this way of seeing. Because the framework is workable in all sorts of contexts, the dots we will be nudged to connect can change our world.

Enterprise Facilitation

According to Enterprise Facilitation, success in enterprise is possible even in the most unlikely circumstances if one convenes three elements. The first is a (business) idea backed by passion, determination, and either know-how or the willingness to learn. The second is a flair for marketing and promotion. The third is financial acumen – accounting, risk assessment, cash flow, scaling up, and so on.

Facilitate convergence of this "trinity of management" and you have a strong foundation for a successful enterprise. Leave out even one of the "legs" of this three-legged stool, and the initiative is compromised – likely to wobble or fail.

Seldom, however, does one person have all three skill sets. The competencies are so different: the type of person with a passion to create a new product or service tends not to have an interest in accounting, and often finds marketing and promotion unpleasant or an uncomfortable effort. When two people get together to start a business, most pairs cover only one or two elements of the management trinity. The same holds true for community initiatives. Community organizations and grassroots groups with a passion to make a difference often lack one or two "legs."

Whether for profit or for community benefit, this way of seeing is as powerful and profound as it is simple.

Origins

Enterprise Facilitation was born from Ernesto Sirolli's reflections on the dismal failure of conventional aid projects he worked on in Zambia in the early 1970s. There, as in countless other places, top-down approaches, too often culturally inappropriate, have wasted billions of dollars. For example, Sirolli worked on a project to grow tomatoes – a food of no interest to Zambians – where farm labourers had to be bribed with beer to participate, and in the end the entire crop was eaten or destroyed in one night by hippopotamuses.

Sirolli found most development aid either patronizing or paternalistic, treating recipients like employees or children respectively. Inspired by E.F. Schumacher's seminal book *Small Is Beautiful,* and determined to find a better way, he pioneered Enterprise Facilitation[1] where the guiding principles ↺ are elegantly simple. (See sidebar.)

Guiding Principles

- Go only where invited.
- Do not initiate anything.
- Listen!!!
- Pay attention to what people want to do – is there an idea backed by passion?
- Remove barriers to success.

Sirolli's passion was to find a way of working such that communities would *invite* him in. No more imposing top-down solutions that were damaging to and disrespectful of the communities they were supposed to serve.

From Schumacher, he learned that, "if you want to be invited, do something beautiful in your own community. Good news will travel fast."[2] And it has: Enterprise Facilitation has been dramatically successful in all parts of the world including Africa, remote Australian communities, and some of the most economically challenged counties in the United States.

Enterprise Facilitator

The strategic element of Enterprise Facilitation is the linking function of an enterprise facilitator: someone passionate about helping people to do beautifully what they love to do. With Sirolli's focus on community economic development, the enterprise facilitator's job description is to show up in town, make it known through flyers, networks, and the local media that they are available to

---

1   Another key influence was Sirolli's study of Humanistic Psychology, and its central tenet that every human being wants to grow and improve their situation. For more on the story of how Sirolli developed Enterprise Facilitation, see the funny and inspiring YouTube video, *Passion, Entrepreneurship and the Rebirth of Local Economies,* in Further Resources, Enterprise Facilitation section.

2   Ibid.

help anyone with an idea for a small business, and wait patiently in local cafés or the town square for people to approach them.

Sirolli is adamant about this point: the idea and energy must come from local people. Enterprise facilitators do not instigate anything. They listen for ideas backed by passion, and then swing into action to help their "client" source local talent for whichever legs of the three-legged stool are missing.

Often all that is needed is knowledge and a bit of mentoring: emerging entrepreneurs seldom fully understand the importance of marketing and finances. For many, simply learning about the "trinity of management" is enough and they are able to access the missing elements through their networks once they know what is needed.

Take aways

Embedded in Enterprise Facilitation are recommendations for anyone with a passion to make a difference. The first and most important is to focus on the trinity of management. Do we have all three elements? What is missing? How can we add it?

Looking more deeply, there is an emphasis on bottom-up approaches: focus your attention and resources on people at the grassroots level who have initiative – those with specific ideas matched by enthusiasm and commitment. Enterprise Facilitation holds that they are present in every community, no matter how disadvantaged or depressed (organizations are a kind of community).

This framework says, "We have everything we need," and that success comes from linking and connecting what is already here – bringing together the three legs. Sirolli also says it does not have to be difficult. The water will flow naturally if we simply remove a few impediments. ☺

The final thing to re-emphasize is the convening aspect guided by the principles of Enterprise Facilitation outlined above. For systems or economies to shift to a higher level, it is helpful to nurture the function that brings the trinity of management together. All the elements may be in the system, but without connecting the

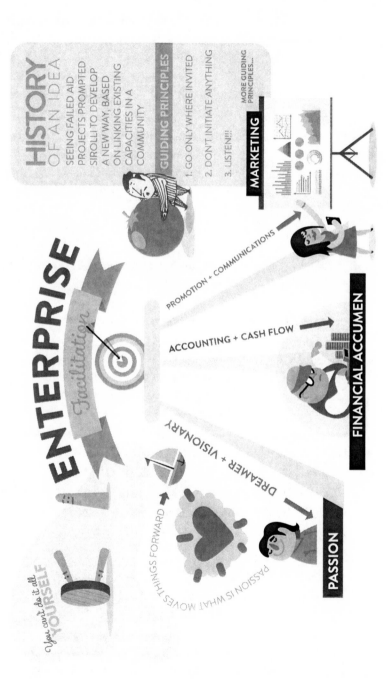

dots, they languish. Find some way to embody the enterprise facilitator role, either by mandating a specific person, or by supporting the networking/linking function in other ways.

Seeing through the Enterprise Facilitation lens

Enterprise Facilitation sheds light on projects and organizations, as well as on change initiatives and social change movements. I suspect that if you run your mind over projects and organizations you have been part of, you too will recognize its power to illuminate situations and clarify why some enterprises and initiatives flourish, and others do not.

Below is a story of Enterprise Facilitation in an economically challenged part of the U.S. I hope it inspires you to use this framework in your local community, and/or at the micro level – in the organizations and initiatives of which you are a part.

Enterprise Facilitation in action

In late 2010, Wallowa County celebrated its outstanding success thanks to a decade of Enterprise Facilitation. Using Enterprise Facilitation in a sustained and inspired way transformed the sparsely populated corner of northeast Oregon into a poster child for bottom-up development.

In a region with a population of under 7500, and an economy based on agriculture, forestry, and tourism, Enterprise Facilitation catalyzed:

- 99 new businesses;
- 170.7 new jobs (and positive impact on a further 549 jobs);
- 68% rate of business success after 5 years (the US average is 25%);
- successful businesses in hamlets as small as 17 people;
- enterprises ranging from cabinet-making and Internet services to physical therapy and adult daycare.

The seed for all this activity was planted by Peter Donovan, a piano teacher and tuner with eclectic interests who lived in the Wallowa County seat – a town called Enterprise (no kidding).

Donovan heard about Enterprise Facilitation in 1998 and instantly knew it would be beneficial for the community he loved. He arranged for Ernesto Sirolli to speak in February 1999.

The locals now look back and laugh. The talk, entitled "Enterprise Facilitation," was hosted in Enterprise; people from Joseph, Lostine, and other Wallowa towns thought they were not welcome! Even with a fraction of the potential audience, there was enough interest to bring Sirolli back in April for another talk on "Enterprise Facilitation." The second event seeded a working group, rigorous training to launch the approach in the county, and eventually a non-profit organization.

Soon after, a search committee reviewed dozens of applications to fill the position of enterprise facilitator. They were looking for someone who embodied the wisdom of Enterprise Facilitation – the potent balance of "initiate nothing, but once approached, help magic happen."

The first person to fill the bill, Myron Kirkpatrick, exceeded expectations, working full-time for the first few years and then gradually scaling back to half- and then quarter-time as pent-up entrepreneurial potential was expressed by community members.

Besides the brilliance of the trinity of management concept, the enduring success of this approach in Wallowa is due to its grassroots origins and ethos. True to the framework, bottom-up passion and drive for the initiative has helped it to be nimble and sustainable, and to avoid the trap of over-reliance on government support. This includes having an active board of 12 local citizens, essential for raising funds to cover the salary of the enterprise facilitator, and also as a gateway to networks of contacts and support for new businesses.

Meanwhile, word of Enterprise Facilitation spread through Oregon and beyond. One ripple is particularly noteworthy: many mining companies are partnering with the Sirolli Institute to boost sustainable economic development in the often remote and challenged Third World communities where they have mining operations.

A key person facilitating this link is Greg Blaylock, a veteran mining industry consultant and an Oregonian who had seen first-hand the effectiveness of Enterprise Facilitation. "I don't think there is a mine or exploration project anywhere in the world that can't use Enterprise Facilitation."

What Greg says of mining towns is true of every community and organization worldwide. There is tremendous untapped capacity – people with viable ideas and others with a natural ability for getting the word out or dealing with the money side of things.

A powerful way to unleash this potential is to introduce a "community initiative facilitator" or an "enterprise facilitator" steeped in the bottom-up trinity of management perspective. It could be you, informed by this framework, and helping to make a few strategic connections. Helping a community or system become better at linking the trinity of management will help a that system help itself, in effective, joyful, sustainable, and empowering ways.

Finer points

- When we do not know what to do – whether in our personal lives or at work – the discomfort and anxiety of not knowing often leads us to "do something, anything." This framework suggests we let inspired passion be the driver. If nothing comes forward in the short-term, have faith that it is not for want of passion and ideas. We have had strong cultural indoctrination to top-down approaches and many of us are disconnected from our passions. Focus on cultivating a high trust environment that makes it easier for people to come forward with their ideas.

- One way to find the "dots" to connect is to host a meeting on a topic of related interest. ↻ For example, Peter Donovan invited Ernesto Sirolli to come to Wallowa to speak. In my own work on food security in a rural region, I arranged a series of four local workshops on growing food and growing food-related businesses, gathered permission to contact attendees, and then offered community initiative facilitation for ideas and projects people wanted to run with.

- The question arises: does there need to be screening for the basic viability of an idea before applying the trinity of management?

The experience of the people in Wallowa County suggests not. They have found that passion is a powerful force, and ideas that most would think not viable have worked out well enough to thrill their instigators. Barring rare off-the-wall proposals, any screening to be done should be for passion and determination.

Backing Passion at Google

Staff at Google have permission to devote 20% of their time to whatever they want to work on. This high degree of autonomy and major backing of innovation (20% of the staffing budget) gives one of the world's largest Internet companies the feel and energy of a start-up. Tapping the passion and creativity of its staff has been the source of such key innovations as Google News and Gmail.

- Most of the Sirolli Institute's Enterprise Facilitators are born and bred in the local community where they operate. Consider empowering one or more facilitative leaders already in your system – those persons in every community or organization who have a passion and flair for helping people connect with others/resources.

- Similarly, the Internet and social media have spawned numerous on-line and off-line ways for people to link and network. Consider how these new platforms can complement and support the enterprise facilitator function.

- Feel free to word the basic concepts to suit your situation. For example, I coined the phrases "Community Initiative Facilitator" and "Community Initiative Facilitation" for contexts where "Enterprise" was too limiting.

Possible pitfalls

- It is a mistake to see bottom-up approaches as the whole answer for problems in communities and organizations. We still need infrastructure and systems that are "top down" – for example, roads and lighthouses, and systems for policing, healthcare, and resolving disputes.

- Some miss the full potential of Enterprise Facilitation by not cultivating strong networks of allies and resources. An Enterprise or Community Initiative Facilitator will be effective to the extent they discover and cultivate webs of contacts to support new initiatives.

- It is easy for the enterprise facilitator role to very subtly become paternalistic and patronizing. It takes mature, egoless personal character to "instigate nothing," and to leave the onus for success with the person who has a passion.

- The very success of this bottom-up approach can get "up the noses" of people steeped in the status quo or vested in more top-down approaches. To mitigate this very real risk, seek out high-level allies and do an excellent job of documenting your positive impact with both data and stories. Know that attempts to undermine your work are not personal. Your success is rocking the boat of others and they are doing what threatened people do. ∧

Enterprise Facilitation has proven the viability of human-scaled, local, and flexibly emergent development. It embodies a paradigm shift – revealing completely different ways forward. Experiment with applying this lens to your business or community endeavours, and share it with others!

At the personal level

I hope you will also experiment with applying Enterprise Facilitation at the personal level. Here are some questions to ask:

- Which of the three legs of the trinity of management best captures my strengths and capacities: passion and know how; financial acumen; or publicity and promotions? The answer to this question offers important insight into how you can serve transformative change in our world. I hope you will honour what comes easily for you. What you can do blindfolded will be a crucial missing piece for someone else.

- How might I be an "enterprise facilitator" for my own passions/ initiatives? Thanks to understanding the concept of the trinity of management, you are in a much better position to gather together the three "legs". To gain access to a missing "leg", perhaps you can partner with others, or barter your services in exchange for what you need. Simply asking for help from a colleague or friend can work too, as most people are very generous with their time and connections in service of helping another's purpose or passion.

• How can I nourish a faith that my passion(s) will bubble up if given a chance? It is not unusual to not know what your passion is. Our culture frequently squashes, discounts, or crowds out authentic interests/passions, and has a strong bias to mainstream rules and roles. It is important to cultivate your ability to sit with the discomfort and anxiety of not knowing, rather than jumping to 'do something, anything.' This is especially true in times of transition. ∞ ☺

• Can I give higher priority to deepening relationships and cultivating diverse networks? This is best when we balance give and take C, not necessarily immediately, but at least over time. Such reciprocity nourishes networks, which in turn begets more connections. The more you help others as they help you, the more you will deepen your ability to facilitate your own and other's enterprises and initiatives. I hope you will value in yourself and in others the crucial functions of linking, connecting, and convening – in aid of beautiful things happening.

Links to other chapters

Both Enterprise Facilitation and Appreciative Inquiry have a deep faith in the passion and potential of people in every human system. The catalyst for Appreciative Inquiry is a person or process inquiring into what is life-giving and ways to enhance it. The catalyst in Enterprise Facilitation is a person or process convening the trinity of management. Take both into your organization or community, and each will strengthen the other.

The simple and profound principles that guide an enterprise facilitator (see page 91) link to Chaordic Design. If your purpose involves shifting paradigms and/or unleashing passion in your family, organization, or community, see whether one or more of the Enterprise Facilitation principles is fundamental to your intention.

Integral Theory points to policies, programs, and structures as a key arena for creating positive change. Enterprise Facilitation clarifies the importance of the convening/linking/networking function for reshaping human institutions to be more inclusive and life-sustaining.

Enterprise Facilitation supports the reorganization phase of the Adaptive Cycle and the rapid prototyping of Theory U: new initiatives/experiments will be more successful if we convene the trinity of management. Theory U, introduced in the next chapter, also shares a focus on what is needed to support a system to evolve to the next level.

Questions

- Do we have passion and determination to see the idea through?
- Do we have savvy for promotion, marketing, and publicity?
- Do we have financial smarts – for managing risk, cash flow, inventory, taxes, partnerships, etc.?
- How can we bring together the trinity of management?
- Are there people and networks already in the system that we can build on?
- How can we cultivate a culture that nurtures and supports one another's passion to contribute?

6
Theory U

Leading from the future as it emerges.
Otto Scharmer

Take a moment to let the above quote roll around in your heart and mind.

It expresses Theory U in a nutshell – a framework for supporting innovation and breakthrough in complex and rapidly changing situations.

Increasingly, I find that my work in community and organizational development calls me to go into new territory. I cannot know whether or how things will work out. At these times, Theory U is an excellent guide. It does not tell me where I will end up, but it offers a clearly defined process to follow – one that gives me solid footing in new situations, and that has helped me do excellent work. With experience, I have come to trust Theory U as I would trust a compass, or a rock climbing safety harness. Having it with me on my journeys, I have been able to take leaps of faith.

I particularly resonate with Theory U's sense that the future is seeking to emerge – that life is emergent, unfolding in wondrous and non-linear ways. It expresses a basic optimism. Yes, the challenges we face are complex and unprecedented, but if we have the courage to go into the unknown, the patience to listen deeply to life, and the willingness to experiment, we can unfold futures better than we could have imagined.

Theory U is also helpful and relevant in everyday situations. It validates my long-standing practice of probing beneath the surface of things – taking time to inquire into what is taken for granted – that has often led to breakthroughs and innovation.

To enhance co-creative leadership in both ordinary and extraordinary times, may you enjoy Theory U's simplicity and robustness! ↻

Sketch of Theory U

To support deep change in our systems and structures, Otto Scharmer, a Senior Lecturer at MIT and the founder of the Presencing Institute, recommends going on a three-phase journey, one that traces the shape of a "U"[1]:

1. SENSING (Beginning at the top of the left-hand side and moving down the "U") – Immerse yourself in current reality. Empty yourself of previous assumptions about how things are. Let go of how you have seen things in the past to be better able to see what is in this moment. Go to places where great things are happening, and observe, observe, observe. + Ask probing questions of a cross section of everyone in the system. Slow down to see things differently, and open your heart and mind. Notice patterns. Go beyond first impressions to see deeper layers of what is.

2. PRESENCING (At the bottom of the "U") – Retreat and reflect. Be fully present – both full with a heightened awareness of what is, and empty with a spacious openness for what is emerging. Be open to seeing and sensing from your deepest source, the way an artist waits on the creative impulse. Quiet your mind, seeking stillness within, and listen for the future that wants to emerge. The more we are fully present and open to what is emerging, the better we

---

1   Scharmer has expanded this sketch into a five-phase journey discussed later in the chapter, but this three-phase description is the core transformative process.

THEORY U

OPEN MIND

OPEN HEART

OPEN WILL

CO-CREATING:
Prototype the New
in living examples to explore the future by doing

CO-PRESENCING:
Connect to the Source of Inspiration, and Will
Go to the place of silence and allow inner knowing to emerge.

CO-SENSING:
Observe, Observe, Observe
Go to the places of most potential and listen with your mind and heart wide open.

are able to hear the whispers of our highest potential. It cannot be forced. One waits, trusting that life wants to happen, attentive to signals. With grace, the energy shifts. Often this comes not as an idea, but as a feeling, a felt sense, or a direct embodiment of something new. Something happens that comes "from a different place," something that expresses the essence of the future wanting to emerge. You (and others, if you are in a group) will know that a threshold has been crossed. ∧

3. CREATING (Moving up the right-hand side of the "U") – Once there is a glimmer of clarity about the desirable future, the next step is to unfold more of it. Scharmer recommends rapid proto-typing. Create a "good enough" prototype, quickly, and get it out into the world. Keep sensing and presencing in relation to this prototype, so that the next generation prototype will be that much better. Do not hold things back, trying to make them perfect before launching them. Keep things moving. Keep learning. Keep adjusting.

Through this three-phase framework, Theory U offers a structured way of moving forward in the face of complex challenges, uncertainty, and rapid change.

When faced with the scary frontiers of the unknown, groups (and individuals!) often carry on with business as usual or get distracted by side issues. Most of current mainstream human endeavour is preoccupied in this way. The principles and guideposts in Theory U are generic enough to work for any complex situation, and specific enough to help groups work coherently and effectively, attending to their situations in ways that help better futures to emerge.

Theory U in action

Scharmer has many excellent stories that illustrate Theory U[2]. I have chosen the one that has had the most impact on me:

---

2   See the Theory U section in Further Resources.

In the late 1990s, Scharmer and his colleague Ursula Versteegen collaborated on a health care project in the Main region, north of Frankfurt in Germany. They were working with a network of physicians who wanted innovations and breakthroughs in emergency care services.

From the outset, Scharmer and Versteegen asked deep questions: *What really was the [physicians'] purpose? Were they there to just "patch people up"? Or were they truly committed to physical, mental, and emotional health? And is this even possible in today's hectic and stressful world?*[3]

...

We began the project by conducting more than one hundred and thirty interviews over several months with both patients and physicians, focused mainly on the doctor-patient relationship. Then we invited the people we'd interviewed to come to a weekend meeting to look at the results. The meeting was held in an old school in the regional capital. Almost one hundred people showed up.

At the meeting, Scharmer and Versteegen shared the interview results, organized into four different levels[4] at which doctors and patients can potentially relate:

1. Transactional: The patient has a broken part and the doctor is like a mechanic.

2. Behavioural: There is an added focus on the behaviours that lead to the brokenness. The doctor might give a list of 'do's' and 'don'ts'.

3. Reflective: The doctor helps the patient reflect on why they are behaving as they are, e.g. teasing out assumptions driving the patient's behaviour.

---

3   All the quotes in this section are excerpts from *Presence: An Exploration of Profound Change in People, Organizations, and Society*, by Peter M. Senge, copyright © 2004 by Peter Senge, C. Otto Scharmer, Joseph Jaworski & Betty Sue Flowers, pages 106-113. Used by permission of Currency, an imprint of The Crown Publishing Group, a division of Penguin Random House LLC. All rights reserved. Any third party use of this material, outside of this publication, is prohibited. Interested parties must apply directly to Penguin Random House LLC for permission.

4   The names for the four levels of care are my own, based on how I understand the key distinctions.

4. Transformational: The most rare and hard to describe, this level involves a kind of letting go, where "the doctor and patient enter into a relationship of mutual influence and vulnerability," and in which there opens up a space for shifting core identity. For example, someone may shift from being a person who is driven and future-oriented, to one greatly slowed down, who is committed to being present moment by moment.

After giving participants time in small groups to reflect on what the four levels meant to them, Scharmer and Versteegen gave participants sticky dots, asking them to use a red one to indicate their current personal experience of the doctor-patient relationship, and a green dot to show what they wanted the reality to be.

> When the voting was over, more than ninety-five percent of all the red dots were at level one and two, and ninety-five percent of the green dots were at three and four. When that picture became obvious, the room grew very, very quiet.

> We pointed out that as patients and physicians, almost everyone seemed to want the same thing – to operate on level three or four – but that what they collectively produced was levels one and two. 'But,' we told them 'the system isn't something out there – you're the system. The system is what you enact.'

Soon, others spoke about how they were encountering the same thing in their own sphere: a mayor, a teacher, a farmer, and more for the whole morning:

> ... gradually there was a huge, collective reframing – not just for individual people, but for the community as a whole.

Then the focus on the past (Sensing) spontaneously shifted to a focus on the present (Presencing). Here's how Scharmer tells it.

> When all of the participants ... saw that they were operating on levels one and two and not on three and four – and not just in the health care system but everywhere – a woman leaned forward and addressed the doctor who'd spoken just before her, saying 'I feel I have to shelter my doctor so that he doesn't get killed in this system.'

Now if you know anything about the psychology of doctors in Germany, you know that they have a high aspiration to alleviate suffering, but they operate in a system that makes it difficult for them to do this. They suffer because what they do is so far from their intent – and the patients also suffer because the doctors often treat them poorly. This woman was enacting the doctors' highest aspirations for how they wanted to act in relation to patients. It was such a simple, heart-felt statement that it opened a space in the conversation. Looking back at it now, I think that it offered a glimpse of how this whole system could operate in the future. It was a moment where the collective field shifted from enacting the patterns of the current whole to uncovering an emerging possibility.

...

At the bottom of the "U", you start to see the future that wants to emerge as people spontaneously enact new ways of being in the moment. We all have our own experiences of this. For me, when I'm part of a social field that has crossed the threshold at the bottom of the U, it feels as if I'm participating in the birth of a new world…. There's a deep opening to my higher Self. ↻ *The movement 'upwards' [Creating] is caused by what begins to come into being through that opening.*

Allowing for emergence, the next intervention was to name the moment:

Okay, everybody can see that we're producing levels one and two. So what initiatives could we undertake that would bring us from one and two to three and four? If there aren't any, we'll just close the session here.

Before long people began to suggest ideas, and by the end of the afternoon, several groups had committed to working together. The projects they formed – including a highly innovative emergency care system – have contributed significantly to the ongoing health development of this region over the [then] four years since the original weekend forum.

...

The day after the doctor-patient forum, Ursula and I and the core group of doctors met to clean up the schoolroom we'd

*been using. We were joined by some patients who'd shown
up, unasked, to help. It was like the morning after a big, wild
party, when you're hanging out, tired but elated, and ready for
whatever happens next.*

Invited to reflect on the forum, one of the volunteer cleaners said
it was like a wedding. For Otto, the volunteer

*had found the perfect words to describe the subtle level of
experience that I'd been unable to express. The day had truly
been about joining two separate elements of a larger field – the
doctors and the patients together in a health care system – in a
way that strengthened both and opened possibilities for each.*

I hope this story inspires you as much as it has inspired me! Imagine this process being replicated for all our complex challenges, including those facing you. The process has already been used by thousands! Indeed, as the next section reveals, Scharmer and another colleague distilled the Theory U framework from the stories of others' peak experiences of innovation and breakthrough.

Origins

Fittingly, Theory U is, itself, the result of a "U" process. Otto Scharmer has a deep interest in organizational learning and organizational change. Early "prototype" versions of Theory U, developed in the 1990s, were greatly enriched by the longstanding collaboration between Scharmer and Joseph Jaworski, co-founder of the Global Leadership Initiative. As part of their work together, the pair conducted 150 "sensing" interviews with leading scientists, and with business and social entrepreneurs, over an eight-year period.

Conversations with these two groups, both at the frontiers of innovation and leadership, revealed an important similarity: breakthroughs in the interviewees' work came from learning to "presence" an emerging whole.

The specifics of how interviewees "presenced" differed greatly from person to person, but the overall pattern was clear. After embodying some version of the first half of the "U," sometimes (not always) something palpably different would emerge "out of nowhere," or in a moment of "grace," or through what Buddhists call "cessation" of normal thinking. Entrepreneurs had clear intuitions about great ways forward, and scientists spoke about different, more intuitive, ways of knowing that gave them breakthrough insight into their work. Ꙩ

Fleshing out this repeating pattern in the interviews, Scharmer and Jaworski articulated it in a series of "rapid prototype" articles and then books, each building upon and deepening the initial offering.[5]

Working with Theory U

One way Theory U has developed is teasing out what Scharmer calls the "five movements of the U process," by adding two more "movements" to the original three – one at the beginning and one at the end. (Feel free to skip to Finer Points on page 115 if you sense that the three-phase version is robust enough for your purposes. You can always come back later.)

He also added the prefix "Co-" to each of the movements. This is to underline how ways forward require our collective leadership and wisdom. ꙨSThe challenges of our time are beyond the capacity of a single person, no matter how capable. We need one another. △

The five movements are Co-Initiating, Co-Sensing, Co-Presencing, Co-Creating, and Co-Evolving.

Here are the five movements, along with a small slice of the ideas for implementation that have been beautifully articulated by Scharmer.[6]

1. Co-Initiating

The first step is to recognize and heed what life is calling us to attend to. Scharmer recommends that we reach out to join

---

5 Delving deeper, Scharmer has reframed the three phases (Sensing, Presencing, Creating) into seven steps, and articulated 24 principles and practices of the U. See Scharmer's book, *Theory U*, in Further Resources.

6 For more depth on these points, see Chapter 21 of Scharmer's *Theory U*.

with others, either by finding those who are similarly called, or sharing how we are called in ways that attract others to join us. Listening together deepens our understanding of the calling, and helps form a diverse core group galvanized by shared purpose and intention. ☺

For example the call might be to improve educational opportunities for children in poverty, or to help small companies reduce their ecological footprint, or to reduce the isolation of seniors. Life calls us to the places where our unique gifts, talents, and experiences can bring most value.

And it calls others to join us.

Here are a few ways to listen to how life is calling you.

* Notice what catches your attention. It might be a suggestion from a friend, a snippet on the radio, or a phrase that leaps off the page when you are reading. When a signal from your outside world matches the core intention of your life, subtly or blatantly, it catches your attention. ∧ Scharmer recommends that we deepen our capacity to catch such signals by reflecting, for a mere four minutes each evening, on "how you interacted with others and what others wanted you to do or suggested that you do."[7]

* Dedicate yourself to reaching your highest potential, and ask to be shown where life is calling you. This is a form of consecration, like taking a vow. The answers may not come immediately, but as we sit with and deepen our dedication, life responds.

* Be open to the call that takes you away from, or adds to, what you are currently doing. This is the definition of a call. It interrupts the status quo, invites us on a journey of becoming, and stretches our understanding of who we are and what we are capable of.

---

7   Reprinted with permission of the publisher. From *Theory U*, 2009 by Otto Scharmer, Berrett-Koehler Publishers, Inc., San Francisco, CA. All rights reserved. www.bkconnection.com, page 380.

Here are some suggested ways to connect with others.

- Look for others who share your interests and seek out those who are doing what is to you the most interesting work. Look "at the margins" as well as to those on center stage. Follow your nose. Get out into the world. Tap into your networks. Consciously break the deeply instilled cultural habit of doing things alone.

- Convene a core group galvanized by shared intention. ☉ Work with attraction rather than promotion, sounding the note of your intention to draw others to join with you. At the same time, consciously reach out to and include a diverse group of people, including those at the margins. ∧ Be open to others shaping a shared intention while at the same time holding true to what is at the core of your intention.

2. Co-Sensing

Once you have a core team with a strong shared purpose, here are some suggested next steps.

- Clarify essential questions that get to the heart of the matter and guide your sensing journey. ☉

- Take learning journeys[8] to "the places of most potential."[9] For example, conduct key informant interviews with people who have been successful in the face of similar challenges. +

- Observe the current system in action and from a variety of vantage points by walking around the organization or company or community, or shadowing people in the system in their daily activity.

- Gather data, find answers to questions that come up in conversations, search the web, keep delving deeper internally (in

---

8   See http://www.presencing.com/tools/sensing-journeys for instructions on how to go on a "learning journey" – an excellent way to gain deep insight into the current reality related to your purpose.

9   *Theory U*, page 389.

the current system) and externally, to find out what others are doing.

- Convene "sensing" events, such as World Cafés, Open Space events, and dialogue sessions. ↻ Create places for broad cross-sections of people to meet and interact with one another. When you get representatives of the whole system in one room, it helps everyone to gain a better understanding of the interconnectedness of a system. In turn, this can foster synergies, and help people find others who share their passion and energy for change.

- Take quiet time to reflect on findings and impressions and what touched you as soon as possible after each interview, event, or site visit. Ask yourself what stood out, what surprised you or was unexpected, and what touched you.[10]

3. Co-Presencing

After a thorough immersion in Co-Sensing, the next leg of the journey is to pause, slow down, and quiet yourself the better to access deeper knowing about the future that wants to emerge. Suggestions for this "movement" are based primarily in ways of being. ○ Prepare a container within yourself for the emerging future, and then patiently hold that space, in faith and trust that that future will reveal itself.

Here are some helpful practices:

- "Let go of your old self and the "stuff" that must die."[11] Let go of past ways of seeing and making sense of things, and let go of control. This is the inner work of creating transformation out in the world. In many respects, this is the most important work, since our own awareness is the source of all that we are able to accomplish. To break through on the outer, we need

---

10 For other excellent questions, see Scharmer's recommendations for Co-Sensing at the Tools tab of the Presencing Institute website: http://www.presencing.com/tools/sensing-journeys.

11 Reprinted with permission of the publisher. From *Theory U*, 2009 by Otto Scharmer, Berrett-Koehler Publishers, Inc., San Francisco, CA. All rights reserved. www.bkconnection.com, page 399.

to let go of the old on the inner. ⊕ This includes letting go of the stories we have about ourselves, our fears, our judgments. ⟳ One powerful way to let go of the old is to say a clear "Yes" to the new that is seeking to emerge through us.

- "Letting come: Connect and surrender to the future that wants to emerge through you."[12] Choose to see from your deepest source, and be open to your highest future potential. Find daily and moment-to-moment practices that help you shift your center of gravity from old small "s" self to the emerging Big "S" Self. Say YES to life. Practices that support accessing your best self include:

  o doing Groundwork, as outlined on page 13 ○;

  o finding a daily mindfulness practice that helps you build the muscle of being fully present and aware in each moment (for example, meditation, tai chi, yoga, chanting, or being in nature);

  o joining an ongoing circle of like-minded people dedicated to supporting one another to live our best future selves.

4. Co-Creating

Once there is a glimmer of the future seeking to emerge, the next step is to co-create a rapid prototype of the essence (perhaps a microcosm) of that future. Here are steps that support Co-Creating:

- "Crystallize your vision and intent"[13] to make a difference in something that matters to you. When we crystallize the vision and 'give it our all', this clarity and commitment help to draw forth the future. Echoing the famous quote by Goethe, it is as if all the elements of the universe line up to help us. Scharmer contrasts this way of being with conventional economics: "If you give all you have and all you are to your

12 Ibid., page 401.
13 Ibid., page 412.

essential project, everything will be given to you. ... This kind of creative or spiritual economy is at the heart of every profound innovation in science, business, and society."[14] ↻

o Key here is to find practices that help you sustain your focus on what matters most, and help you keep distractions and diversions at bay. For example, do not feel bound to respond to all requests and emails, and reserve chunks of time during your best hours of the day for moving forward on your top priorities.

o Look for the seeds of where your desired future is already manifesting, and find ways to build and amplify those, rather than starting from scratch. +

• Form core groups. One person alone is limited in what s/he can do. Four to five people working together for a shared purpose are almost unstoppable.

• Create prototypes that are microcosms of the future you want to create. It takes a fraction of the time and effort to develop a solid first-cut than it does to develop a polished complete offering. Share prototypes when you sense you are 50-80% of the way there. This way you can gather helpful feedback and learn quickly and easily what works and what does not. Scharmer speaks of these early prototypes as "landing strips for the emerging future." He also notes that the process of creating prototypes involves multiple mini U processes, even on a daily basis – Co-Initiating, Co-Sensing, Co-Presencing, and so on – to stay attentive to, and in service of, the future seeking to emerge.

5. Co-Evolving

A current frontier for all of us is creating institutional and social infrastructures that support ongoing innovation and transformation. Our institutions and organizations need to go beyond "one-off" breakthrough initiatives.

---

14   Ibid., page 413.

Co-Evolving helps "U" principles and practices become embedded in our institutions and organizations. For example, creating opportunities for people to "see and act from the emerging whole" – not through top-down dissemination of rigid models, but through cultivating relationships, trust, and capacities to see and sense the systems we are part of in support of breakthrough innovations.[15] ⟲ ⟳ In other words do collective Groundwork ○: cultivate the 'social field' of our organizations and institutions, the way organic farmers cultivate the soil.

Sometimes, all five movements will be important; at other times, the core three will be enough. In either case, you may experience – like me – that Theory U validates, gives names to, and extends ways of doing and being that you have already been working with. I hope you will experiment further with Theory U, mindful of the following finer points and possible pitfalls.

Finer points

- The future is seeking to emerge always ∧, and not only when we are using Theory U as an explicit collective process. It can be very helpful to cultivate your ability to sense what Scharmer calls the 'social field', and especially shifts in the social field. For example, those moments when a group's energy shifts from fragmentation and separation to being more unified and collected. By bringing our attention to such a shift we can help it to unfold more fully: energy follows attention. By sharing what we notice we help to grow the ability of our systems to see and sense themselves.

- The most important step in Theory U is Co-Presencing, at the bottom of the U. It is here that we shift from being anchored in the past, to being attentive to the future seeking to emerge. To pass through the eye of the needle into the emerging future, we need to let go of our cherished assumptions, judgments, identities, and ideas. To create breakthroughs in the outer world, we need first to break through internally. ○

---

15 Ibid., pages 425-442.

- Commitment is central to our ability to break through internally. Being half-hearted or merely going through the motions does not activate the dynamics of the U. Life responds to us exactly to the degree we show up.

- All the commitment in the world, though, does not make things happen at the bottom of the U. Sometimes things unfold at breakneck speed. Other times we must be patient, holding space a long time before something new emerges. We can create conditions supportive to Co-Presencing, but we cannot force it to happen.

- When we are engaged in something deeply meaningful and working on it intensely, breakthroughs often come in the shower, or while we are taking a walk. In other words, become fully saturated in the situation and then take a break by stepping away from the computer, desk, or meeting room. ↻

Possible pitfalls

- A weak starting point – such as a weak statement of purpose or core question – compromises the whole U process. It is important to reflect deeply. What are we really trying to accomplish? What has most meaning? ↻

- Another possible pitfall is losing focus. The Co-Sensing phase opens up many issues and different ways of understanding a situation. Stay aware of and focused on your core purpose and open to the possibility that there is something deeper seeking to unfold. In other words, do not shut out the possibility of refining your purpose, but take care that it is not diluted.

- Lack of diversity compromises U processes. We are more comfortable with people who are the same or similar to ourselves, and yet the likelihood of a significant breakthrough is greatly enhanced by cross-pollinating with people who see things very differently. ∧

- One serious potential pitfall is disregarding the future seeking to emerge because initially it seems too alien to embrace. When something is radically different, it can be hard for us to entertain it as a real possibility. We balk, not wanting to go into such foreign territory. One way to avoid this potential pitfall is to pay extra attention to the perspectives of people at the margins, since they are freer from attachment to the status quo, and so more likely to bring forward a radically new pathway. ∧

- Consider the balance of divergence and convergence when moving through the U. Seek a wide range of perspectives and voices when Co-Sensing (divergence) but not so wide that you dilute the primary purpose of the process. When doing rapid prototypes, narrowing down to only one area might be just right, or it might be taking convergence too far. By reflecting on the balance of divergence and convergence, we may get a feeling for what best serves our purpose. ∞

At the personal level

Like all the frameworks in this book, Theory U is something we can live on a day-to-day basis, and living it strengthens our ability to see and sense both our current reality and emerging possibilities.

Most of the "Working with Theory U" section (pages 109-115) applies at the personal level. I hope you will take the time now to consider your own life from the perspective of the practices and suggestions outlined there.

Here are a few additional recommendations for making Theory U a way of life.

- Set a clear intention to live your highest potential. Make a vow, in your own words, to live your life fully. ○

- Annually or quarterly reflect on what your emerging future is calling forth in you. Recommit to living to your highest potential.

- Join or create a circle with others committed to living their lives guided by the future seeking to emerge through them. Being in a face-to-face circle that meets weekly, monthly, or quarterly is one of the most powerful ways to support your emergence. ↻

Ask others to lovingly call you out when they see you living in either "same old, same old" ways or "absencing" as described in the Absencing text box.

- Have a daily "presence" practice, such as meditation, tai chi, yoga, or chanting, and explore whether there are inner work tools[16] that work for you.

- Practice sensing shifts in group energy such as the times when the group comes together in a more unified "field." Your personal relationships are a great place to develop this sensing muscle. The more you are attuned to shifts in group energy, the more you can nurture this same awareness on the part of colleagues and others in your larger social system contexts. And the more you will be able to name Co-Presencing in the moment.

- Take time to "be" in nature – beside a river or next to a tree or anywhere that helps you feel the current of life. Being in the wilderness, or even a garden, can help us come home to what matters most to us. It helps to still the chatter so we can pick up deeper signals. ↻

Abundant, generative, and sustainable life wants to happen through us. As systems and old ways of doing things continue to break down around us, it is increasingly important that more people know how to step away from fear, panic, and despair, and choose to support radical breakthroughs by attuning to the generative future seeking to emerge.

Links to other chapters

Theory U is fundamentally trusting, appreciative, and purposeful. As such, it is closely linked with Groundwork and the first two frameworks. For example, every phase of the U benefits when a high level of trust O supports people to show up fully and share

---

16 See Sutherland, Kate. *Make Light Work: 10 Tools for Inner Knowing.* Vancouver, British Columbia: Incite Press, 2010. Chapters on Flirts, Automatic Writing, Inner Guides, and Guiding Image can be particularly helpful.

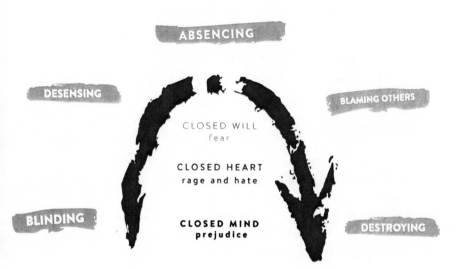

ABSENCING

DESENSING

BLAMING OTHERS

CLOSED WILL
fear

CLOSED HEART
rage and hate

BLINDING

CLOSED MIND
prejudice

DESTROYING

Absencing

Scharmer names that in the face of the disruptions of our current times each of us has three main options: muddling through, moving backwards, or moving forward. Presencing is a pathway for moving forward. Muddling through is doing the same old things, and Absencing is the name Scharmer gives to moving backwards.

Presented visually, Absencing is the opposite of Presencing. Instead of diving deeper into what is and exploring the future seeking to emerge, Absencing is about being blind to what is, cutting ourself off from anyone outside of our chosen echo-chamber, and being cut off from ourself. Instead of an open mind, heart and will, we are closed at these three levels. Each of us exhibits these tendencies to some degree. Scharmer contends that the more we have capacities for seeing and sensing systems, and the more we have the tools and supports for Presencing, the less likely we are to Absence.

Source: Scharmer, C. Otto. *Theory U: Leading from the Future as It Emerges (Second Edition)*. Oakland, Califormia: Berrett-Koehler Publishers, Inc. 2016, page xxix.

their unique gifts and perspectives.

Here is a sample of the links to other frameworks:

- Enterprise Facilitation helps scale up prototypes.
- The big picture perspective of the Adaptive Cycle can create a great rationale for embarking on a U process.
- Generative Dialogue distinguishes Co-Presencing (Flow) from three other types of group interaction, and offers insights into how to cultivate it.

With experience, you will soon see more ways that Theory U links to other chapters, including the next one on Process Oriented Psychology. For starters, Process Oriented Psychology helps Co-Sensing and Co-Presencing by cultivating awareness of what is unfolding moment by moment, and by calling us to embrace what we would rather turn away from.

Questions

- Is Theory U an appropriate framework for this issue/context? Is there openness to new ways of doing and being?
- What is the most powerful way to articulate what we are trying to do?
- Where are places of highest potential that we can learn from (Co-Sensing)?
- Am I in service of, present to, and open to the future seeking to emerge?
- What is seeking to emerge?
- What rapid prototypes are most likely to bear fruit and support scaling up our work?

7
Process Oriented Psychology

From wonder into wonder existence opens.

Lao Tzu

I was blown away the first time I saw Process Oriented Psychology in action in 1992. It was as if I had been moving sand with a tea-spoon, and someone gave me a shovel.

More than 25 years later, I am still in awe of the transformative power of this framework. I value how it helps me name dynamics as they unfold moment by moment in *any* group context, and how seeing more clearly has guided my actions at home and at work. Indeed, I use this lens on a daily basis, and consider it one of the most versatile and potent in the book.

It is also a framework that has called me to be more curious and present to the mystery of life. It has helped me to be comfortable with being uncomfortable, and to reap a thousand gifts and rewards that have come when I turn towards people, situations, and feelings I would rather run from.

Its clarifying and empowering perspective informs everything from my efforts to grow as a person to how I engage as a global citizen. Perhaps it will be as fundamental for you.

Origins

Arnold Mindell has long been charting the territory of individual, group, and societal processes. Since the mid-1970s, his Process Oriented Psychology has been especially helpful for understanding the dynamics of power, marginalization, and change.[1]

Mindell's theoretical framework, often called Process Work, is rooted in Taoism, Physics, Jungian Psychology, and more recently, Shamanism. It is a big picture way of seeing – positing that the patterns of behaviour at the group level are also played out at the individual level and at the level of society and humanity as a whole, and moreover that these different levels are not separate at all, but rather richly inter-penetrating. ⊕

Process Oriented Psychology

Process Work's central focus is on *process*, defined as the constant flow of information. What is emerging in this moment? ↻ What new element or elements are unfolding? What dynamics are in play?

Would you like to understand what happened at the meeting yesterday? Would your group be wonderful if you could just get rid of one person? Is your organization sluggish or stuck? Do you repeatedly notice ageism, sexism, intellectualism, or some other form of social ranking?[2]

Process Work is rich with concepts to help you understand and navigate in groups, and also in your personal life. The most fundamental of these is the distinction between primary and secondary process.

Primary and secondary process

Primary process is what we identify with. It is how we like to see ourselves and how we want others to see us. The secondary pro-

---

1   Many other people have been integral to the development of Process Work's theory and practice. Foremost among these is Amy Mindell, Arnold's wife, for naming "metaskills" – compassion, patience, loving kindness, etc. – as crucial complements to the analytical framework and concepts described in this chapter.

2   Process Work is not against rank, or power. It supports the voices that want us to be more aware of rank and of power, and to be more conscious in their use.

cess, moment by moment,[3] is that which we experience as "other": what we don't want to see in ourselves or have others see in us.

Some examples can be helpful.

For the most part, in North American society, the primary process is rational and scientific. A typical secondary process is intuitive and emotional.

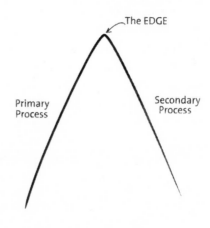

Primary Process

Secondary Process

The EDGE

At the group level, by and large, male, white racial values and perspectives are primary, while female, and/or black, indigenous and people of colour values and perspectives are secondary. At the individual level, being neat and well-organized might be primary, and being lazy and confused might be secondary.

The natural tendency is to bolster our primary process: we resist or marginalize what is secondary, since by definition what is secondary challenges or disturbs us.

A key goal of Process Work is to help individuals and human systems to be more aware of their secondary processes. For example, I identify with being logical, practical, and effective. I disavow my spontaneous, wacky side. Process Work helps me be more aware of what I am marginalizing and supports me to cut loose and have more fun.

Similar to the distinction between figure and ground on page 10, we will *always* have a primary and a secondary process. We cannot avoid it. No matter how much we grow and develop, there is always what we identify with and what we experience as "other." When we identify with failure, we marginalize success,

---

3 "In a sense, your secondary process doesn't really exist. It is a process. It is fluid and changes. Talking about a secondary process is a momentary description of a momentary experience. It is a snap shot." Email communication with Stanford Siver.

and if we embrace success, we marginalize failure, and so on, and on, and on.

The goal is not to get rid of the secondary process (much as the primary process would like to). The goal is to be ever open to where life is taking us – and therefore open to it taking us over the "edge" between our primary process and the secondary process in this moment, and now in this moment, and again now in this moment. ↻

Doing this connects us to the flow of what is most vital and life-sustaining. This may not be comfortable but it feels right.

The edge

The *edge* is the boundary between the primary and secondary processes. When I am well inside the edge on the side of primary process, I am in the familiar territory of what I consciously identify with as being me. At the edge, I am likely to exhibit what Mindell calls "edge behaviour."

People have different responses to the edge, (and the same people have different responses at different times). Some go silent and withdraw, while others talk incessantly or joke around. Some get very irritable, blaming, and aggressive, and others get weepy, hysterical, or spacey. The constant is some degree of discomfort, often with a "hot potato" dynamic: energy looking for an outlet.

It is very powerful, both personally and for work with others, to be more aware of the edge and the patterns of edge behaviour. Being able to name the dynamic, "I think we are at an edge," can help us ride the waves of awkward silence, high emotion, or swirling thoughts. Simply knowing that I have an unexplored spontaneous side helps me slip over into new territory when I reach the edge of that frontier.

Signals

The main way to be aware of secondary processes and edges in yourself and in a group is to pick up on what Mindell calls "signals."

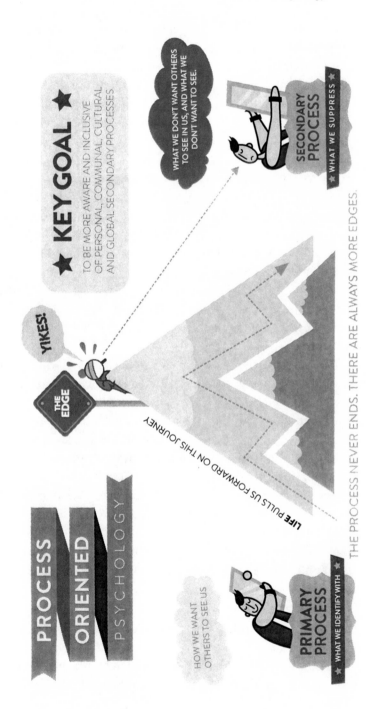

Signals convey information about a process. They draw our attention away from the comfort zone of the primary process, and indicate that there is something else going on. They may occur internally in the form of gut feelings, intuitions, inner voices, or the body's sensations and spontaneous movements. They may also occur externally in the form of body language, tone of voice, synchronicities, and relationship dynamics.

Signals are often subtle and easy to miss. However, when we choose to pay closer attention, it gets easier to notice them. The best way to become better at picking up signals in group contexts is to be aware of our personal primary and secondary processes. That helps our receptors to be uncluttered and open, and helps us get our personal agendas out of the way so we can better see/ sense what is emerging.

Signals can come on multiple channels: through speech, body language, dreams, and intuitions. There can also be signals from the wider field: a phone ringing, a bird at the window, a snippet on the radio, a passing siren.

Important signals to look for are double signals – where there is incongruence between what a person or group says or stands for, and what else is going on. A person might say, for example, "I'm delighted to meet you," but there is a double signal if their arms are crossed tightly across their chest. The primary process is delight; the secondary process might be fear, distrust, or anger.

If you notice a double signal in yourself, in another person, or in a group, get curious about it. Mindell says, "Behavior makes sense." Trust that there is a good reason for the double signal, and bring warm, curious awareness to the situation. This will help people be more aware of the process, which in turn helps the process to unfold in positive ways.

The field

Another concept central to Process Work comes from physics: the *field*.

Imagine a handful of iron filings scattered on a piece of light cardboard. Now imagine that you bring a magnet to the underside

Photo credit: Windell H. Oskay, www.evilmadscientist.com

of the cardboard. If you did this in school, you will remember how the iron filings moved into a symmetrical arching pattern around the poles of the magnet as shown in the image above. Move the magnet and the iron filings move too, revealing the "field" created by the magnet.

Relationships, groups, and societies also exhibit field dynamics: shift one aspect, and other factors in the field shift too, in patterned ways. Change the physical environment, and group dynamics shift. Remove the leader of a group and the remaining people jockey around until the leadership vacuum is filled. C

Roles

Mindell uses the concept of roles to help explain what happens in the field. A magnetic field pulls iron filings into different positions. A human field pulls people into different roles.

Have you ever had the feeling with a family member or intimate partner that you are being taken over by an energy vortex? If one person is occupying the role of *successful* and *together,* that can leave you with some variation on *confused* and *hopeless.* Perhaps you are sucked into the role of *abandoner* due to your partner's deep-seated story of being the *abandoned one.*[4]

---

4   Process Work also invites us to go a layer deeper. If your partner remains stuck in the role of "abandoned one," it can be as if your partner somehow abandons you – s/he is not fluidly moving out of the role, and so is not fully available to engage with you in your relationship.

One person strongly playing out any specific role, will, like the magnet, create a field that pulls other people into different complementary roles. The field does not "make" people take on certain roles, but it does create a tendency for those roles to be expressed. Which group member takes on a given role depends on each person's characteristic or momentary proximity to the role and their level of awareness.

Process Work maintains that you cannot really say where the dance of roles starts. You cannot blame it on the one person who first expressed a particular role, although that may be where you first noticed a process. From Mindell's perspective, it is as if a more complex process created a certain atmosphere in the relationship field, and then people started to dance with the atmosphere and were pulled into different roles. Moreover, each of us is influenced by multiple overlapping fields in every moment, based on our backgrounds, life circumstances, and current context.

The intent of Process Work is to increase our awareness of what is. The more we can remove the filters of blame and judgment, the better we are able to see. ↺

Stepping in and out of roles

Our language is revealing: people "step into" the leadership role. It is like putting on a costume, or accepting a role in a theatrical production. Stepping into any role tends to pull us to perceive, feel, and behave in prescribed, almost formulaic, ways.

Classic roles identified in process work include *listener, appreciator, oppressor, victim, marginalizer/excluder, terrorist,* and *saboteur.* Each of these roles has a "field" because it has been played out in human societies for millennia. By implication, when a person steps into the role of victim (or victimizer) they are swept into patterned ways of seeing, being, and behaving that have been created and reinforced by human societies. This can be momentary, or long-term, depending on circumstances and awareness.

An aware person is able to resist the pull of a field in order to make conscious choices about how to be and what to do in a group context. Being aware of field and role dynamics, and speaking about them explicitly can burst their thrall, and free individuals in a relationship, group, or organization to choose their responses more consciously.

Roles are not bad. They are like gravity. We cannot avoid them. Roles become problematic if people are unconscious about them and in them. Ideally, in Mindell's view, we have the awareness needed to move fluidly between roles: stepping into and dropping roles as circumstances change.

There is also a natural fluidity to roles. Expressing one role shifts the field, and can pull others into different roles. Oppressors become oppressed by their oppression of others. Caregivers become needy of care. Role switching is an organic part of most processes.

Formal leader versus leader as role

Process Work distinguishes between the designated leader, such as the boss or CEO, and leadership as a function that can move around in a group. For example, if someone speaks against the designated leader's misuse of power, the person speaking out is also occupying the leadership role, at least momentarily.

Disturber and elder

Mindell's work highlights two roles for special attention: *disturber* and *elder*. The disturber is the one who challenges the primary process in a group, implicitly calling the group to embrace a secondary process it would rather not deal with. As such, the disturber role is very important to the overall health and wellbeing of our relationships, organizations, and societies. At the same time, like an auto-immune response, the primary process in groups will usually do its best to block or get rid of the disturber.

The *elder* role cares for the wellbeing of the group as a whole and everyone in it. One common form of eldership is to stand for the inclusion of people and perspectives that are marginalized. At the same time, this very important contribution of eldership is only part of the picture. According to Stanford Siver, an experienced Process Work practitioner, "Eldership sometimes means: supporting, momentarily, one-sided exclusion; supporting the dominant group, culture, or members; and even occasionally an elder might support her own momentary one-sidedness. 'Yes to hearing the voices of the marginalized group but No, not like that.'" Process Work is a refreshing challenge to formulaic political correctness.

The more awareness there is in a group, the more likely it is that different people will take turns playing the role of disturber, or expressing the disturber role for different issues and aspects of group life. Similarly, the eldership role will move around or can be held by multiple people in different moments, based on their different backgrounds and sensitivities.[5]

Mindell's idea of the *field* helps us understand how a disturber vacuum can draw others to disturb the status quo in the same way that a leadership vacuum can draw others forward into a leadership position. Healthy groups have disturbers. Indeed, if the disturber role is temporarily suppressed or blocked, groups will become less effective and more tense or "edgy" due to unexpressed secondary processes.

Rank and privilege

Another core concept in Process Work is *rank*. Perhaps thanks to our animal ancestry, humans tend to rank themselves and others in a complex web of pecking orders. Social ranking is part of every human system, C and is implicit in the distinction between primary and secondary processes. Different cultures and sub-cultures rank the same things (wealth, weight, education, etc.) in different ways. Universally, though, we assign higher rank to what is primary – internally, in our hearts and minds, and externally, in our relations with others.

How you rank in a specific context will be the sum of different kinds of privilege. For example, you might have structural privilege, by virtue of being the boss, or you might have psychological

---

5   All roles are non-local, in that they move around from person to person(s). A role does not only appear in one person ... even if it might seem so in the moment.

privilege in that you greet each day feeling optimistic. Other main categories of privilege identified by Mindell are: social (education, connections), economic (income, wealth), health (weight, fitness), and spiritual (sense of belonging, inner peace).

Each of us is a mixed bag, ranking higher on some aspects and lower on others. For example, a person might be well-educated (ranking high), but have a mental illness (ranking low). A person might have a strong sense of identity (ranking high), but live in poverty (ranking low).

The blessing in these multiple dimensions of privilege is that each of us has a window into the dynamics of rank. In the areas where we rank lower than others, we have personal experience of what it feels like to be "second-class."

Think of your own situation: where do you rank high (according to the standards of your culture/sub-culture), and where do you rank low? What differences do you notice between these two positions – for example in your overall wellbeing, your sense of belonging C , or your awareness of others?

Privilege-induced blindness

Mindell observes a significant consequence of the way we are wired for ranking: "Privilege makes you blind." For example, when you are white in North America, you are relatively blind to your own privilege, and to the experiences of people of colour. Perhaps your attention tends to focus on other white people. When you are an adult at a party, you may tend to visit with other adults, skipping over youth or children as irrelevant to your interests. The criteria might change, but not the process of seeing some as higher and others as lower, and of being relatively blind to what you define as "lower."

The blindness due to privilege means people and dimensions with lower rank (as in whatever is secondary in a group) often bring critical missing perspectives to social systems. ⊃ Think of the biting commentary of teenagers. We often have acutely good vision when we feel that others with higher rank are not using their privilege well.

This is not to say that people with lower rank see the whole picture. While they have an ability to see parts of the whole field missing from the mainstream's view, they also have their edges to their own secondary processes. For example, marginalized people often feel powerless and may not appreciate how powerful they actually are, and marginalized people can themselves be ageist, sexist, classist, etc.

Rank and privilege in groups

Privilege-induced blindness is a key factor in group dynamics. Take this classic scenario of "turning a blind eye":

- Individuals in a group politely raise a disturbing issue, expressing a "secondary process".
- When other individuals ignore the issue, it is marginalized by the group's "primary process."
- Individuals politely raise the secondary process issue again. The primary process again ignores the issue.
- The secondary process raises the issue more forcefully. The primary process can no longer ignore the issue, but turns a blind eye.
- The secondary process stridently raises the issue. The primary process says that it will only listen to the secondary process if it presents the issue in a "reasonable" manner – that is, politely.
- If the secondary process raises the issue politely, the primary process ignores it.
- And so on, until individuals continue to escalate, amplifying the secondary disturbance to the point where there is a shift in the system.

This is a very human dynamic. It plays out in all the nooks and crannies of society, and at all levels: within individuals, relationships, groups, organizations, societies, and the whole human field.

Deep Democracy

Matching the scope of these dynamics of privilege, in the late 1980s Mindell began to explore and define a guiding principle that he called "Deep Democracy":

> Unlike "classical" democracy, which focuses on majority rule, Deep Democracy suggests that all voices, states of awareness, and frameworks of reality are important. Deep Democracy also suggests that the information carried within these voices, awarenesses, and frameworks are all needed to understand the complete process of the system. Deep Democracy is an attitude that focuses on the awareness of voices that are both central and marginal.[6]

Deep Democracy calls us to embrace what is secondary, not only in terms of social groups and their issues, but first and foremost in ourselves! The more we bring awareness and acceptance to our secondary process, the more we can be present to the primary and secondary processes of the group (i.e. relatively free of having an agenda for things to go one way or another). From here, Deep Democracy calls us to be present to and to embrace all the ways a human system receives signals about what the secondary processes may be. This includes listening for and valuing different states of consciousness, synchronicities, dreams, body sensations, and "those voices that seem to come from beyond space and time."[7] ↻

The following reflections were written by Lane Arye, a therapist steeped in Deep

Other ways of seeing

Separately and together, the concepts introduced in this chapter offer rich perspectives on group dynamics. The Mindells have other great concepts, such as time spirits, ghost roles, and metaskills. Please see Mindell in Further Resources if you would like to delve more deeply into the Process Oriented Psychology framework.

---

6 Deep Democracy Institute, www.deepdemocracyinstitute.org/deep-democracy-explained.html, used with permission.

7 Stanford Siver, "Deep Democracy," http://stanfordsiver.net/deep-democracy/

Democracy and Process Work, as a contribution to the Occupy
Wall Street (OWS) movement.[8] The "story" is longer than most
as different parts speak to different people, and there is nothing I
want to cut. As you read it, see how its gems of wisdom apply to
your current context(s), including family, classroom, workplace,
or community.

Process Work in action

A Therapist Talks about the Occupy Wall Street Events

Last night I [Lane Arye] was talking with a group of
activists/organizers from around the country about their
impressions of the Occupy Wall Street (OWS) movement.
They were curious how the insights of a therapist and
conflict facilitator schooled in Worldwork[9] (which was
developed by Arnold Mindell) might be useful to folks
in the movement. After our teleconference, the activists
encouraged me to write this.

First off, OWS is surrounded by a host of critics, from
long-time social change organizers to mainstream media.
We can learn from critics in at least two ways. They can
help us improve by pointing out what we genuinely need
to change. Paradoxically, they may be criticizing us for
something we actually need to do more congruently.
Seen from this angle, critics may be highlighting strengths
we don't yet know we have.

---

8 The Occupy Wall Street movement developed in the summer of 2011 in response
   to an article in Kalle Lasn's Adbuster Magazine suggesting that America needed its
   own Tahrir Square (a reference to the Arab Spring protests in Egypt). Before the
   actual occupation began on September 17, 2011 in Zucotti Square, close to the
   Wall Street financial district in New York City, the movement had agreed to use
   general assemblies to make decisions rather than typical leadership/spokespersons
   models. A key slogan was, "We are the 99%," as distinct from the wealthiest top
   1%. The main prompts were the increase in income inequality, especially in light
   of bank bailouts following the 2008 financial crisis, and the extent of corporate
   influence on the democratic process. By October 9, there were "Occupy" protests
   in over 600 communities across the US, and in dozens of cities around the world.

9 Worldwork is a body of work within Process Oriented Psychology which says that
   to understand the psychology of individuals, it is important to understand their
   wider context – including the "world" issues of racism, homophobia, economic
   and social marginalization, sexism, etc.

Take one criticism: The General Assemblies (GAs)[10] lead to a kind of individualism of people wanting to be heard and contribute, unaware of the impact on the thousand people listening. In one recent GA, a small group of frustrated men hijacked the meeting, cursing and physically threatening the entire assembly. Even in less dramatic situations, most GAs are filled with judgment, fracturing statements, and individuals repeating each other just so they can get themselves heard.

From one point of view, the criticism is valid. Yes, Western individualism can be very problematic and it is always a good time to learn to be more communitarian. But perhaps there is also something beautiful about this individualism. People have the sense that they can finally speak up about the economy, that their voice is important, that they do not have to shut up and listen to talking heads who supposedly know better.

It can be useful to think about this in terms of roles. (Just as an actor plays many different roles, we all play different roles in our lives, sometimes without awareness.) Individuals wanting to be heard at a General Assembly might be in the role of someone who wants attention. "Pay attention to me! I have something to say!" For years, our "democratic" system has ignored these voices. They have been excluded by money, a political system that merely offers citizens a chance to vote, and a financial system bent on inequality. But now this role is finding a public voice.

This role is talking to another role that does not listen. Many bankers, politicians, media and others are part of the role of "not listening." In essence the voice says: "Shut up! I am not listening to you!" (Though they have learned to be more subtle: "I wish the protestors had a single message.")

There must be a third role here – the listener, who holds the space and receives what someone is offering.

---

10 See Footnote 8. The OWS "General Assemblies" (GAs) embodied a radically different way of organizing. Instead of decision-making by a few top-down leaders/designated spokespeople, all decisions were made by consensus at daily GAs. This was both a tremendous strength of the movement, and a great challenge. The GA experience is relevant for any group or community that seeks to be authentically inclusive of all voices. See the Conscious Co-Creation chapter and the Coda for more thoughts on how to help groups make decisions and achieve unity of purpose in a timely way.

Perhaps facilitators, organizers and activists could benefit from knowing that these three roles are around. For example, when someone is talking a lot at a General Assembly, the facilitator could echo back what the speaker is saying, getting to the essence of it so the speaker knows she/he is heard, and perhaps so the speaker knows what she/he is trying to say.

I have seen this work around the world. During a forum for reconciliation in the Balkans soon after the war there, a Bosnian Croat would not stop speaking, holding a virtual filibuster, despite the impassioned pleas of his fellow participants. When I echoed back what I thought he was trying to say, he thanked me and sat down. When people feel heard, they stop demanding the time to speak, because filling the missing role of the listener addresses the core need of the one who has something to say.

Of course, doing this can be challenging. Everyone wants to speak, but who can really listen? In Worldwork we say that the elder is the person who can listen to all voices, who supports everyone to speak and be heard, who wants the best for all sides of a given conflict. OWS, like the rest of the world, needs more elders.

Another way to make this useful is to think that probably everyone needs to be heard, and everyone needs to cultivate the listener. Having large groups move into pairs or groups of three people who can actively listen to one another about a given topic might be one way to meet this important need. Occupy Minneapolis used this with huge success during a consensus process that had been routinely blocked. After pair-sharing, the group was able to move forward. Or Aussie facilitator Holly Hammond has found value in "asking people to raise their hands in response to some questions e.g., 'Raise your hand if this is your first General Assembly' (very useful information!); 'Raise your hand if you camped at City Square'; 'Raise your hand if you were present at the eviction', etc." Both methods let people know that someone was listening to them, interested in them, and that they were an important part of what was happening.

This is one reason, by the way, that the spokescouncil model can be effective. In that model there are affinity groups – embedded small groups so everyone can speak – and they each send representatives who sit at the spokescouncil, like spokes of a wheel. Each spoke can consult with its affinity group and the whole process is done in public so it marries transparent representation and participation.

Similar to the listener is the appreciator. At some GAs people are attacked when they step into new roles of leadership. How much more exciting it could be if these brave souls were cheered when they took the risk to lead. One OWS activist came up with a different solution: put up a large chart where people can leave anonymous (or signed) messages of appreciation for people in the camp. It is another way to model that people are hearing!

The one who wants attention is related to the role of the one who wants to contribute. Even long-time organizers may find themselves not knowing how to contribute to this movement that has its own culture, that may not seem to them to be strategic or sustainable. They might feel disempowered as well, and feel they have to adapt to the General Assembly culture and the rules that have been set up by the OWS organizers. And those who anticipate that the long history of oppression will be repeated yet again may feel that their voices and contributions will not be as welcomed.

When we notice the companion role, the one who receives someone's contribution, then we find ways to work with this dynamic. For instance, facilitators might again try getting people into small groups, and having folks take turns saying what they personally feel they have to contribute to this movement. The other people in the small group can draw them out, and encourage them to find ways to bring their unique gifts. Many people want to contribute, but do not know how. It is important to support people to find their strengths and fulfill their need to contribute. This can prevent people from feeling discouraged or disempowered (and thus prevent harmful consequences like deciding not to return, or discouraging others from engaging with the movement). It also breathes new life into a movement by bringing new ideas and energy from the grassroots.

When I mentioned this point to the social change organizers, they put it to immediate use. One young woman of color from

New York was talking about her frustration that, while People of Color have shown up, their contributions have often been minimized. She felt that OWS needs just the opposite – to value and prioritize these contributions in order to continue expanding and diversifying the movement. Another Philly organizer of color drew her out, asking how she imagined making a difference. Her initial hesitancy was transformed into excitement as he appreciated and received her great ideas. Then he asked if she would like coaching on one point, which she welcomed. A week later she facilitated a 100 person POC [Person of Colour] meeting, as well as a media training for POC/women, teaching them to better find their voice, initiate interviews, and speak up in the media. She also had other projects/contributions in the pipeline. As she wrote, "My mind and my heart are a-whirlin."

Here was one great example of what I imagine are a multitude of potential contributions that could be supported to come forward if we notice and fill the various roles in the field.

Let's not forget that the man who wanted to hear her ideas also made a contribution of his own. Filling the role of the receiver was itself a contribution!

He had been one of those experienced organizers who had not found a way to be of use to the OWS movement. He had at various times tried to give advice to OWS facilitators about how to have better GAs and create a more sustainable movement, without having had much impact. Now he realized he had been stuck in the role of the one who speaks (one of the many well-meaning people who turn into advice givers) rather than being an elder. That is when he decided to try something different. (It is important to note that after listening to her, he asked if she wanted coaching, then waited for her feedback before offering his own ideas.)

Another way to look at all of this is through the lens of a criticism that has been leveled by the mainstream media at the OWS movement – that it has so many heads and no unified message. Rather than looking at the truth or falsehood of this criticism, let's see if there is something good about it! If OWS is a creature with many heads, then anyone can be the head. When so

many heads are singing beautiful songs, it is up to each of us to
both listen, and to sing our own song. The most beautiful and
compelling ones will be heard. From this perspective, we are all
potential leaders of this movement.

According to Mindell's idea of Deep Democracy, when all voices
and roles have a chance to be heard and interact, the wisdom
of a group or community can arise. Perhaps the many-headed
creature that is OWS needs our particular song, our particular
direction. The world is trying to express itself. It is using us.
By believing in our own voice, in our own special part, and by
actively listening to our peers, we can help the wisdom and
power of the movement to develop.

Process Work, as the above story illustrates, has much to offer
groups and organizations of all types. Who, for example, has not
been part of a meeting where many want to be heard and few are
listening? Who has not, at one time or another, wanted to contribute but not found a way to do so?

Through key concepts such as role, field, and secondary process, Process Work helps us to be more aware and to make choices
that support enlivening unfoldment in our relationships, groups,
organizations, and societies.

To be masterful with Process Work takes years of dedication.
Even so, there are countless benefits from getting your feet wet
with the concepts and ideas in this chapter. Try sharing them with
a buddy from work or a significant other to quicken your understanding. In doing so, you will cultivate sensitivity to unfolding
processes in yourself and in groups. Whether you go for mastery
or for basic knowledge, here are some finer points and possible
pitfalls to be aware of.

Finer points

- We might not understand why a person or group behaves as
  they do, but Process Work says we can take it on faith that if
  we better understand their context, the field, their primary and
  secondary processes, etc., even violent and destructive behaviour will make sense. For example, if a sub-group has been

marginalized or ignored whenever it uses due process and official channels, it has little recourse but to escalate to more "disturbing" behaviours. I value how Process Work has helped me look more closely and open my mind and heart more fully in challenging situations.

- The basic stance of Process Work is curious, compassionate, fierce, and courageous. It has both a receptive "yin" of acceptance and acknowledgment of what is, and an active "yang" of standing for inclusion of all voices and perspectives, even if what is marginalized is the perspective of an elite! Process Work is too big for a "politically correct" box. Rather, its allegiance is to the mystery of the all-embracing and ever-unfolding process of life. ↻

- Process Work calls us to be mindful when defining agendas and priorities for group endeavours. Too often, issues are framed in ways that exclude secondary processes. It is best when the agenda is truly inclusive, for example, of the issues frontline workers have with how things are going as well as the CEO's agenda. ↻ ↺

Possible pitfalls

- Avoid the tendency to judge yourself harshly when you become aware that you are at the edge of a secondary process. Instead *appreciate* yourself for being willing to acknowledge what you had previously stuffed out of sight as unacceptable. + Taking yourself up to and over an edge is like rocking your own boat. It shakes up your (primary) identity, in a good way, and can make you more humble. Remember that every one of us ever and always has edges. You cannot not have secondary processes. And the more you open to what is secondary, the more you will be in flow with all of life. ↻

- It is edgy to talk about the edge. If you introduce a group to the concepts of primary process, secondary process, and edge, there is a good chance this will take the group to an edge. Some people or one person might be confused, agitated, or compelled to crack a joke. A minor pitfall is to miss this great opportunity for group members to reflect together on how the energy feels in that "edge" moment.

- It is a misunderstanding of Process Work to say that we should always cross an edge. Maybe it is too much to cross the edge at this time, or maybe it is enough just to peek over the edge. Some edges should not be crossed (for example, if you have an edge to being violent). Others are long term processes, for example, where we approach the edge, maybe put a toe over it, and come back to breathe and reflect on the whole scene before feeling our way into what is next. Toastmasters is successful at helping people become public speakers in part because it identifies a gently graduated sequence of steps to take (or edges to cross) in one's own timing.

- Naming a person or group as the disturber can lead to scapegoating: "Everything would be fine if we could just get rid of JJ." Our very human desire to block what upsets our primary process can lead us to misuse the framework. We take the concept of "disturber," together with the general agreement that disruption is "bad," as justification for excluding or blocking an individual or group. This is the opposite of what Process Work intends. Process Work calls on us to get curious about what disturbs us, trusting that it offers us greater aliveness, freedom, and effectiveness. If you see scapegoating starting to happen, consider stepping into the role of disturber yourself. By bringing out your own personal expression of the energy, even momentarily, you can diffuse the group's impulse to scapegoat "JJ."

- Do not misunderstand Process Work as always calling for us to keep "JJ" in our group. "Divorce" is also a process. What Process Work does recommend is that we deal consciously with the energy carried by JJ, since s/he simply took on a role that emerged from the field. For example, suppose the disturbance is neediness. How might the energy of neediness be useful to the group? In addition, it may be that if other group members acknowledge their own neediness, JJ will be freed up to move out of that role. If JJ continues to be a problem despite the group's best efforts to integrate her or his message, it may be that JJ's process is to go in a different direction.

- If you sense that your contribution is a disturbance for the groups you are part of, there is the very real possibility of push-back from the primary process, in the form of exclusion, humiliation, sidelining, ridicule, excommunication, and more. Here are a few tips for this possible pitfall.

  o Go into situations with your eyes wide open. Do not expect people expressing the primary process to like you.

  o Do not take things personally. Different fields are influencing everyone. You and others are playing parts in multiple wider dynamics.

  o Set an overarching intention: "May I contribute to the group's process in ways that serve the highest." ○

  o Be mindful of what is primary and secondary for you personally in the situation, moment by moment.

  o Be humble. Know that you have been on the other side of this dynamic in another circumstances. Sometimes you are the one suppressing what is secondary!

  o Take time to get to know people as people, one-on-one if possible. + Reach across the divide by choosing loving kindness over righteousness or aggression. ↻

  o Get creative about supporting others to see what they are disavowing. Use questions that invite them to see your perspective.

  o Be curious. Have no idea what will unfold. Do not hold others in specific roles. Allow space inside you for things to unfold in unexpected and non-linear ways. ↺

- Our privilege makes us blind, and what is in our blind spot is likely among the most generative and transformative elements of the picture. ✛ An antidote is to ask ourselves, "In what way am I blinded by privilege in this situation?" Two other great options are to work with a colleague to help each other see blind spots, and to create practice opportunities for each of you to step momentarily into unfamiliar roles.

- Spiritual rank can be associated with subtle possible pitfalls. For example, people who are consciously on a spiritual path may take this stance: "I am above all this; I have graduated from being consumed by coarse emotions and material matters; I am well on the way to enlightenment." The very real benefits of spiritual practice are often closely linked to this kind of arrogance. Instead of supporting greater love and compassion for all that is, some spiritually privileged people use their insight to keep themselves separate and disconnected from other people, and other species.

At the personal level

According to Process Work, our personal process cannot be separated from the wider processes of which we are a part. We are affected by the fields of the groups we belong to, the issues and concepts we identify with, and the wider societal forces at play, to name just a few.

Put another way, "I am part of the system." And more pointedly, "I am part of the problem."

This is a humbling shift of perspective and stance. We are asked to step out of the ego-comforting roles of being the (outside) helper, expert, or saviour in shining armour. Instead, we are invited to dance in the messy, more vulnerable, and uncertain dynamics of owning our part in the systems we aim to change.

One of the more succinct statements of this shift comes from an Aboriginal activists group in Queensland, Australia based on wisdom distilled from their activism in the 1970s:

If you have come here to help me, you are wasting your time.
But if you have come because your liberation is bound up
with mine, then let us work together.

I hope you will join me in making this a central plank of how you work for positive change: let us truly take on board that each of us is inextricably part of the systems we aim to change, and therefore that our work at the personal level is integral to our work in wider spheres. For one thing, this helps to overcome righteousness – a key impediment to our ability to influence others!

This chapter is seeded with invitations to explore how Process Work applies at the personal level. I hope you will reread the chapter from time to time, and that you will make it an ongoing practice to reflect on:

- How my personal process is part of the process of the wider system I aim to influence.

- My primary processes – how I want others to see me, and my secondary processes – the behaviours, people, or circumstances that make me uncomfortable, uneasy, irritated or triggered.

- How I tend to feel and behave at an edge, in terms of body sensations, body posture, emotions, and thinking patterns, and ways to grow my ability to be curious, compassionate, and courageous at the edge. O

- My rank/priviledge in economic, social, health-related, psychological, or spiritual dimensions/categories. How might my privilege make me blind to the experiences and needs of others?

- The roles I tend to take on (or *not* take on), such as disturber, rule enforcer, victim, or leader, and opportunities to grow my ability to move fluidly between roles.

- Opportunities to cultivate my eldership and grow the ability to listen for and hold space for all the voices and energies in the systems of which I am a part.

- How I can get better at picking up signals – both interior signals such as my body sensations, body movements, and intuitions, and exterior signals such as an interruption, an insect, or a sudden burst of sunlight?

I hope these reflection topics help you to integrate the Process Work framework into the very fabric of your being. If you are like me, your life will be the richer for it!

Moreover, when we do "our own work", it becomes part of the solution to the wider issues we care about. The field effect makes it so. And what we learn at the micro level will help us have compassion, wisdom, and experience to draw on in larger processes. C

Links to other chapters

Process Work is an all-encompassing framework. There are always multiple layers of unfolding processes, including within an individual, at the micro level of a single conversation, and all the way up to the macro level of international relations. As such, Process Work brings depth to every other framework in the book.

For example, Process Work shines light on Groundwork's spectrum of fear and trust: as we open, thanks to higher levels of trust, more of what has been secondary comes forward.

When one or more people in a group feel comfortable enough to say what they really see, feel, or want, this can help a conversation evolve from Politeness to Breakdown as outlined in the Generative Dialogue Framework. Process Work calls our attention to marginalized voices, and to body sensations and synchronicities. This helps us to be more conscious of what is taking place, and therefore more able to strengthen the container in ways that deepen conversations.

Process Work and Systemic Constellations both highlight rank or social order in systems, and both invite us to see how the "field" shapes what is happening in our groups, teams and organizations.

The next framework is Ken Wilber's Integral Theory. Like Process Work, it is a big picture lens, richly comprehensive and insightful for work at all levels and in all sorts of contexts. There are dozens of ways that Process Work complements Integral Theory and vice versa. Read on so you can discover these for yourself.

Questions

- In this moment, what is primary and what is secondary – in me, and in the group?
- Can I sense the field? Am I being pulled into a particular role? Are others being pulled into roles unconsciously?
- Are we at an edge?
- Is there a disturber? Is the disturber also speaking for me, at least in part? Can I own and express my part of the disturber role?
- What do I take for granted? In what ways am I blinded by privilege? (These are important questions no matter what our life circumstances!)
- Is there a need for eldership? Can I value all voices?

8
Integral Theory

Delight in the paradox of things being both wholes,
and parts of bigger wholes.

I have great respect and appreciation for Integral Theory. Of the ten tools, I think this one is the "sharpest" – it offers by far the most distinctions and dimensions, and the most comprehensive overview. If I want to be sure I am not missing something when working with groups, I look with an Integral lens.

My brother introduced me to Ken Wilber's book, *Up From Eden,*[1] in 1984. The book's core idea is that human consciousness is evolving, and in a specific sequence of levels. I am grateful for how precisely Wilber has mapped this and other aspects of consciousness in his extensive writing. A better understanding of how to shift consciousness is a powerful lever at this critical time in human history.

Thanks to Wilber's work, I am also able to stand more strongly in support of inner work. Wilber documents our tendency to overvalue what can be seen, touched, and known through scientific observation – and to undervalue and ignore interior dimensions

---

1   Ken Wilber. *Up From Eden: A Transpersonal View of Human Evolution.* Boulder, Colorado: Shambhala Publications, Inc., 1981.

such as intention, cultural beliefs, and consciousness. As well, I appreciate and echo his strong criticism of "flatland" – the blind alley in contemporary Western society that shuns hierarchy so vehemently that it loses crucially important distinctions of value.

Integral Theory is like an icebreaker – it opens up passageways in territory previously less accessible. This framework has helped me become more self-aware and more conscious of different perspectives and dimensions in the groups I work with. I hope you enjoy the learning journey it makes possible.

Integral Theory

The title of another of Wilber's books describes his work well: *A Theory of Everything.*[2] For the past 45 years, Wilber has developed and refined a way of mapping all the dimensions of consciousness into one framework – from subatomic particles to galaxies, from every "ology" in the social sciences to business, ethics, and spirituality. His Integral Theory is a map of maps that systematically charts all aspects of human knowledge about consciousness, and thereby shows how parts of the picture relate to other parts and to multiple definitions of "whole."

Integral Theory is brilliant for shining light on aspects of the picture we are blind to. ∧ This is crucially important if you or your group want higher levels of wellbeing and effectiveness. Being more "Integral" is a potent strategy for personal and organizational growth. The more we know this in our bones, the more we are able to overcome our natural tendency to turn away from what we would rather ignore, and to address the parts of the picture we have neglected. ∧

The full framework is nicknamed AQAL,[3] which stands for "all quadrants, all levels" and further includes "all lines, all states, and all types." Here is a taste of a few fundamental concepts.[4]

---

2   Ken Wilber. *A Theory of Everything: An Integral Vision for Business, Politics, Science, and Spirituality.* Boston, Massachusetts: Shambhala Publications, Inc., 2000.

3   AQAL is pronounced "ah-qwul."

4   This taste of Integral Theory offers only a basic introduction. For more, please see the Integral Theory section in Further Resources.

Holons

Wilber builds upon Arthur Koestler's idea of a *holon*. Holons are "wholes that are simultaneously parts of other wholes, with no upward or downward limit."[5] For example, an organization is both a whole, and part of the local community. In turn, the local community (a whole) is part of a region, which itself is part of a country.

Atoms are a part of molecules, which are a part of cells, tissues, organs, bodies, etc.

Why is the concept of holons important?

We have a tendency to see parts *or* to see wholes. Both are too partial. Both miss the fundamental inter-relational, 'whole/part' nature of the universe. We cannot fully understand the forest without understanding trees – its component parts. The story of that forest is equally not complete without seeing it as part of a bioregion, and so on. We need to get better at seeing the interconnections of the systems within systems. ∞ C

Training ourselves to think "holonically" helps us avoid the twin dangers of collapsing and totalizing. It invites us to be nimble – to see wholes where we otherwise would collapse everything and see only parts, and to see parts when we would otherwise sweep up everything into wholes, masking important distinctions, interconnections, and possibilities.

What holons have in common

In different ways, both Koestler and Wilber identify four fundamental tendencies of all holons – self-preservation, self-adaptation, self-transcendence, and self-dissolution. Here is Wilber's formulation:

> **Self-preservation:** "All holons display some capacity to preserve their individuality, to preserve their own particular wholeness or autonomy ..."[6]

---

5   *From Sex, Ecology, Spirituality* by Ken Wilber, © 1995, 2000, page 35. Reprinted by arrangement with Shambhala Publications Inc., Boston, MA. www.shambhala.com.

6   Ibid., page 40.

Self-adaptation: "The *partness* aspect of a holon is displayed in its capacity to accommodate, to register other holons, to fit into its existing environment."[7]

Wilber speaks of the preceding two capacities as agency and communion. "As a whole, it remains itself; as a part it must fit in." These opposing tendencies are a "primordial polarity that runs through all of manifest existence," named by Taoism as the yang and the yin. Similar to Taoism, Wilber observes that health calls for self-preservation and self-adaptation to be in balance. Too much of either leads to pathology.[8]

Self-Transcendence: Under certain circumstances, "different wholes ... come together to form a new and different whole. There is some sort of creative twist on what has gone before."[9]

The newness cannot be reduced to agency and communion. There is something more. Something has emerged: "... the universe has an intrinsic capacity to go beyond what went before."[10] ↺

Wilber characterizes agency and communion as a horizontal dimension, and self-transcendence as a vertical dimension that opens up new horizontal dimensions of agency and communion.

Self-dissolution: "Holons that are built up (through vertical self-transformation) can also break down."[11]

This is the opposite of self-transcendence and, intriguingly, Wilber cites overwhelming evidence that holons dissolve in "the same vertical sequence in which they were built up (only, of course, in the reverse direction)."[12]

Over all, though, Wilber sees a universe that is evolving. Molecules emerged out of atoms. Nations emerged out of tribes. There is a trajectory towards ever more complex systems that

7   Ibid., page 41.
8   All quotes from Ibid., pages 41-2.
9   Ibid., page 42.
10 Ibid., page 44.
11 Ibid.
12 Ibid.

"transcend and include" the preceding holonic systems. Life wants to happen!

Dynamic tension

Take a moment to reflect on these four capacities in your own life. See if they ring true. Do you sense the opposing tugs of agency and communion – for example, how the more you express your uniqueness, the more challenging it is to fit into a larger system? And, vice versa, the more you adapt to a system, the less you express your individuality? ↺ ∧ C

Health or resilience, as in a great marriage, is having these

Translation vs. Transformation

Wilber names two main types of change. Translation is change at the same level of agency and communion. Transformation is when something new opens up, thanks to a holon self-transcending to a higher level. Most change initiatives are merely translation. To have major and lasting impact, aim for transformation.

two tendencies in dynamic balance – being "both my own wholeness and part of something larger, without sacrificing one or the other."[13]

What about self-transcendence? Does it resonate for you that under certain circumstances, something new emerges, and that this newness allows agency and communion to occur at a new level? The emergence is non-linear. There is a breakthrough, and suddenly a whole new set of possibilities opens up.

At the same time, self-transcendence requires overcoming the pull of self-dissolution. It takes effort. The conditions have to be right. If conditions deteriorate, a marriage – for example – can fall apart.

Recognizing the "whole-part" nature of life, and the four fundamental tendencies of holons, helps with understanding ourselves and groups. In particular, it calls us to be aware of competing tensions – to stretch to be fully ourselves and simultaneously fully in

---

13 Ibid., page 45.

communion; fully accepting of the cycles of dissolution and fully trusting, open to, and having faith in what is emergent. ↺

Take the following story, for example.

Exchanging Murder for Youth Leadership – Part 1

Marilyn Hamilton, a skilled community and organizational consultant, "lives" Integral Theory. When I asked her for a story to illustrate holons, she shared work she has been doing in her home community of Abbotsford – the thriving hub of a food production community an hour east of Vancouver, Canada.

Marilyn had asked herself what would motivate her to bring her skills to a research project focused on creating a welcoming and inclusive community.

Her answer was to change the headlines. In 2010, local papers noted that Abbotsford had the dubious distinction of being the "murder capital of Canada." Four youth had been killed in six months, all victims of drug-related gang wars. Marilyn wanted to change the story to, "Abbotsford is the youth leadership capital of Canada."

It was a bold goal. Good people in her community had been working for many years to turn things around for youth. Multiple dedicated efforts had not been successful.

Enter holons! Steeped in Integral Theory, Marilyn and the research team (the Team) knew to look within the "whole" called "Youth" for its many "parts."

Her first step was to engage a diverse group of youth to gather data from their peers. Her team included native speakers of English, Punjabi, Korean, Mandarin, and German – matching the main culture groups of the local community. The survey included six questions. When sorted by postal code, language, faith community, age, and gender, it allowed Marilyn to document more than six subgroups within the "youth" and general population, each with distinct preferences, perspectives, and needs.

It took months of persistent offers to be able to present her findings to local authorities. Then the data spoke eloquently:

"one size fits all" public institution youth programs were not working. Marilyn remembers the local Fire Chief saying, "Now I understand that the values of Punjabi speakers differ from those of Korean or English speakers and why we have to adjust our presentations to what is important to each cultural group."

Having helped the wider system appreciate the parts within the wholes called "Community" and "Youth," Marilyn's fellow team members then worked to create the conditions for different subgroups of youth to realize their natural capacity for self-transcendence.

To better understand the rest of this story, you need to know about the Four Quadrants, one of the most important and best known aspects of Integral Theory.

As you explore this second layer of the framework, see how it complements and deepens your understanding of holons. Then in turn, see how understanding holons and their four capacities deepens your understanding of the Four Quadrants.

Four Quadrants

The Four Quadrants are created by the intersection of two fundamental distinctions: individual vs. collective, and interior vs. exterior.

The individual vs. collective distinction echoes the earlier exploration of holons. It says that when we reflect on a situation, we need to look at it both from

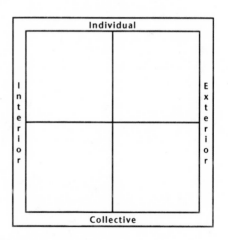

the perspective of individual people/trees/atoms/etc., and from the collective context: groups of people/forests/molecules/etc. In other words, everything has both individual dimensions and collective dimensions. We need to look (and take action!) from both perspectives.[14]

The interior vs. exterior distinction is equally, if not more, crucial. Interior refers to inner or subjective aspects such as motivations, intentions, values, cultures, likes, and dislikes. Exterior refers to dimensions we can touch or point to in definable ways. This includes physical actions that manifest our reality, as well as corporeal aspects of life such as forests, cities, garbage ... and social reality: networks, organizations, and social systems such as governments, policies, courts, and contracts.

The resulting four fields are summarized in the chart below.

	Individual		
Interior	**Interior-Individual** **"I"** **Intentional** **(subjective)** Thoughts, emotions, memories, states of mind, perception, and immediate sensations	**Exterior-Individual** **"IT"** **Behavioural** **(objective)** Material body (including the brain) and anything you can see or touch (or observe scientifically) in time and space	**Exterior**
	Interior-Collective **"WE"** **Cultural** **(inter-subjective)** Shared values, beliefs, meanings, language, relationships, and cultural background	**Exterior-Collective** **"IT"** **Social** **(inter-objective)** Social systems, structures, processes, networks, technology, organizations, government, and society	
	Collective		

14 "Everything is a holon." This means that an element in the "Interior-Individual" quadrant is itself both a part and a whole. For example, a certain individual's subjective preference for pesto is part of that individual's system of subjective preferences for Italian food. There are multiple and branching series of nested holons in each of the four quadrants!

To live fully, and to support growth and positive change, we need to engage with all four quadrants. This is one of the most powerful ways we can create conditions for self-transcendence for our holon self, and for the groups and organizations we care about.

Other applications

The Four Quadrants are useful in other ways. Here are a few applications and benefits.

- The Four Quadrants can be used as a checklist, prompting one to see a specific situation or thing from four distinct and complementary perspectives. In particular, it helps us value both what we can know empirically, and what we can only know through introspection or intuition. ∧

- It helps group members to understand and value one another's very different perspectives. For example, Jasmine is focused on cultural values and Sandy is focused on individual action. Both are important and valid perspectives. They complement each other! The truth of one does not lessen the truth of the other.

- It helps open up a discussion when an individual or subgroup claims that, "It all boils down to X" – usually Individual-Exterior. When dealing with complex issues, it is common for an individual or subgroup to collapse the four quadrants into one, usually the one they personally have the most affinity for. The four-quadrant framework is a great way to say, "You are right, and these other people are right too." Often simply drawing the grid shown on page 153 is enough to help people hear one another better, and to value the gifts in the perspectives of others. ↻

- It names and acknowledges the interior dimension. Our scientifically-based industrial society has greatly undervalued the power of intuition, intention, values, beliefs, vision, and meaning. ∧ ↻

- It also names and acknowledges the exterior dimension. The self-help/therapy community often gives relatively little value to action in the collective sphere!

Part 2 of Marilyn's story below shows how she used the four quadrants as a diagnostic tool, to help her understand a critical gap in how her community relates to youth. △

Exchanging Murder for Youth Leadership – Part 2

Marilyn's research had diagnosed a profound lack of capacity in the Lower-Right quadrant (Exterior-Collective). There was no meaningful place for youth to have a voice in the structures and policies that influenced their lives. The youth were disenfranchised.

To turn this around, the Team intervened in three ways. They:

1. convened conversations that allowed youth with similar interests to find each other;

2. provided information that allowed youth to value themselves, their situation, and their possibilities;

3. provided modest seed funding to support youth to implement their own ideas.

The other key element the Team provided was deep trust that transformative initiatives would emerge naturally if the youth were given time, space, and encouragement to create their own. "We had to hold the space a long time," Marilyn made a point of adding, noting that emergent processes are not linear and do not conform to prescriptive timelines.

So far, the youth have launched three initiatives, each rippling out in positive ways. A year-end story in the Abbotsford News noted that the previous 12 months had been murder-free. Marilyn and her team like to think that their activities in 2009 contributed to this outcome.

The moral of the story is "work integrally" in order to have transformative results – attentive to all four quadrants, and to the whole/part dimensions of your situation.

Four quadrant theory of change

Integral Theory says that to be effective, change initiatives need to work on all four quadrants. For example, health programs focused on individual action (upper right – Exterior-Individual) will be more effective if they:

- link to what individuals care about
(upper left – Interior-Individual);
- tap into cultural values and norms
(lower left – Interior-Collective);
- are supported by social systems and structures
(lower right – Exterior-Collective).

Similarly, a change initiative aimed at changing values (upper left – Interior-Individual) will be more effective if it includes support to take specific actions (upper right – Exterior-Individual), and so on.

Change initiatives based in any one quadrant will be stronger and more effective if they expand their scope to include the other three quadrants. Here is another story to illustrate this important point.

Integral Theory in action

In 2005, Maureen Jack-LaCroix dedicated her skills and capacities to "the Great Turning."[15] She retired early from her successful career as Creative Director and Producer of large-scale events to devote herself to the core question, "How can we best support people to lead more environmentally sustainable, socially just, and spiritually fulfilling lives?"

She knew intuitively that how she worked needed to embody the values and principles of what she wanted to create. So it is fitting that she called her organization the Be The Change Earth Alliance, echoing Gandhi's quote, "We must be the change we wish to see in the world."

Through rapid prototyping, Maureen and her team developed a replicable three-stage program centered on community "Action Circles." See pages 158-9 (Integral Approach) for how she shared inspiration from Integral Theory to introduce the action circles to participants.

---

15 The phrase 'The Great Turning,' as coined by eco-philosopher Joanna Macy, refers to the creative response and shift in values currently underway from an industrial-growth society to a life-sustaining civilization. It is running parallel to 'The Great Unravelling' of planetary life support systems due to industrial abuse of the natural world.

Integral Approach

In designing the [Action Circle] program, we have been inspired by Ken Wilber's Integral Approach (Wilber, 1999). This proposes that to transform individuals and societies we need to be working simultaneously in four fields of the human experience: the individual and the cultural, internally and behaviourly. This translates in the *Be The Change* program in the following way.

Circle members:

Read excellent resource materials that offer important information and perspectives about climate change, voluntary simplicity, raising healthy children, sustainable living, and similar themes. These resources support us as we evaluate our priorities and values that guide our decisions, accept responsibility, and increase our motivation to make changes in our behaviour. (Upper Left)

Interior - Individual

INTENTIONAL

I

Connect with other people through participation in a committed circle process — an element that we believe is fundamental to re-weaving community and shifting our culture from disengagement to connection. We need to understand our interconnectedness and the oneness of the universe. One of the most powerful ways to make this shift is by experiencing the support, insight, connection and power in being with others in a circle. (Lower Left)

WE

Interior-Collective

CULTURAL

Exterior - Individual

BEHAVIORAL

IT

Take action in our personal lives each week, to lower our ecological impact and increase our contribution to the happiness and wellbeing of ourselves, others and our communities. We then report back to the circle for peer accountability – one of the few things that consistently works to support people to make lasting change.
(Upper Right)

ITS

SOCIAL (SYSTEMS)

Exterior - Collective

Act Collectively It is not enough to clean up our own act. We also need to be shifting our collective systems – our institutions and social systems. While Be The Change is strictly non-partisan and does not take policy positions as an organization, we do urge circle members to take action at the collective level. We also provide a list of possible actions that the circle can do as a group, and how to connect with other circles to create a network of change in your community.
(Lower Right)

Source: Be The Change Earth Alliance. *Participant's Action Guide.* Vancouver, British Columbia: Be The Change Earth Alliance, 2008.

The Be The Change team also routinely uses the four-quadrant framework to ensure their work follows the Integral model. For example, when selecting forty community leaders to host conversations at a conference, they made sure each quadrant was represented by at least six speakers and circulated the speakers through the delegates seated at round tables. In this way, delegates were stimulated to consider their lifestyles and community systems from all four quadrant perspectives.

Similarly, when Maureen adapted the Be The Change program for use in high-schools, she explained the Integral model to teachers. Time and again, Maureen has had positive feedback from those teachers about the value of addressing each of the quadrants in their environmental education sessions. When students take time to clarify their own values (upper left), and recognize the industrial-consumer cultural influence on their lifestyles (lower left), they see how the global environmental issues (lower right) are connected to their local lifestyle choices (upper right). From this clear perspective, youth feel empowered to make different choices (upper right) and often become strong advocates for change in their homes and schools.[16]

To experience for yourself how powerful the four quadrants can be, take a moment now to reflect on a current challenge or opportunity from these four distinct perspectives. I suspect you will gain insights that will help you on your way. To speed your learning and use of this framework, see the following finer points and possible pitfalls.

Finer points

- When you create a team/board of directors/conference/group process, ensure that every quadrant is well represented.

- Everything in this chapter is just a portion of the comprehensive map of consciousness that Integral Theory has to offer. Other helpful distinctions include states, levels, lines, and

---

16 Over the five years of program development in local classrooms, 17,000 students took approximately 100,000 actions, reducing the amount of CO_2 in the atmosphere by 500,000 kg. Source: Be The Change Earth Alliance.

types, each of which could have a chapter of its own. If you are curious to know more than the thumbnail that follows, please see suggested reading in the Integral Theory section of Further Resources.

o **States.** There are many states of consciousness, including waking, dreaming, and deep sleep. $\wedge$ $\circ$ You may have experienced different states as a meditator. Yoga, intense physical activity, or dance can induce altered states. Many of us have had brief peak experiences such as feelings of bliss, oneness, or deep peace. States are transitory, and generally we experience many different states in a single day. The mere fact that we experience different states can give us a glimpse of the different levels of consciousness named in the next bullet.

o **Levels.** There are patterned stages of consciousness such as the cognitive and moral developmental stages that children pass through as they grow up. Levels are not transitory the way states are. Each level "transcends and includes" the preceding levels. People at lower levels do not have access to the perspectives and capacities of people at higher levels. There are hundreds of different ways to define levels, including, for example Trust Theory's analysis of ten levels of trust.[17] Another is a potent four-stage model often cited by Wilber – egocentric, ethnocentric, world-centric, and kosmocentric – that shows how the more developed we are, the larger our frame of reference.

o **Lines.** There are many different lines of development, such as cognitive, ethical, emotional, spiritual, aesthetic, and physical. Distinguishing lines helps us see how we are all "mixed bags," more developed in some areas and less developed in others. For instance, contrary to what many of us assume, just because someone is smart does not mean they are morally developed, and so on.

---

17 See pages 35-36 of a chapter on Trust Theory at http://ow.ly/hI5s30dOFav

o **Types.** There are many "horizontal" differences in the type of consciousness, such as masculine versus feminine. Jung distinguished introverts and extroverts, intuitives and sensates, etc., now popularized as the Myers Briggs system for classifying personality types. There are dozens of other typologies that articulate different "flavours" of consciousness as distinct from levels, lines, and stages.

- Use a variety of "modes" in your organization or group. The classic Robert's Rules of Order type meetings favour the Exterior-Collective quadrant and largely ignore the interior dimension. By including inner work approaches such as meditation, guided visualizations, and guiding images, you can bring the left-hand (Interior) quadrants into the picture. Similarly, mind mapping and visual images draw out intuitive, non-linear ways of knowing to complement the rational logical style of thinking that is currently so dominant. ∧

- There is tremendous latent potential in the untapped passion, good will, and capacity in our organizations and communities. △ Working integrally helps us access these discounted or devalued energies and contributions. Beyond how meetings are structured, how does your group or organization support Integral approaches to the challenges it faces?

- A great way to get started with Integral Theory is to dive in. Do not let its depth and breadth get in your way. Pick one aspect, like the quadrants or holons, and use it for a single task, such as planning a meeting or debriefing a project. Getting your feet wet is a great way to experience the power of the Integral lens. With that under your belt, add another aspect. Do not be surprised if you are soon swimming along. The framework can feel like a lot to integrate at the outset, but it is so helpful and makes so much sense, it may soon become a constant companion.

Possible pitfalls

- While the framework splits "everything" into quadrants, lines, stages, etc., the deeper point is that all these dimensions are

INTEGRAL THEORY

To be Integral you need to address all four quadrants.
Here are integral Theory's four dimensions
for supporting greater health.

INDIVIDUAL

INTENTIONAL:
WHAT PERSONAL VALUES
AND MOTIVATIONS?

BEHAVIOURAL:
WHAT INDIVIDUAL BEHAVIOURS
LIKE SLEEP AND DIET?

INTERIOR ← → EXTERIOR

CULTURAL:
WHAT CULTURAL VALUES
AND NORMS?

SOCIAL:
WHAT POLICIES, STRUCTURES,
AND SYSTEMS?

COLLECTIVE

integral to each and every aspect of what is. For example, while the framework helps to value and validate the interior dimension, it is not about devaluing or invalidating the exterior dimensions. See the following sidebar, for a simple example of how feeling hungry is Integral: you cannot eliminate a quadrant. The quadrants make important distinctions AND at the same time are co-existing and completely interpenetrating.

- Watch for being too cerebral and losing connection with your heart. Integral Theory, especially the full framework, can captivate the mind. It is easy to get caught up in analyzing. Remember that love, wisdom, and compassion are as important for being effective in groups as clarity of perspective.

- People unfamiliar with Integral Theory will not understand terms like "holon," "upper left quadrant," and "Interior-Collective." These helpful distinctions are jargon to someone who does not know or relate to the framework. Be mindful: make sure your shorthand conversations do not exclude people. ↻ ∧

- Naming levels of consciousness can be controversial and even insulting to some. People can get very defensive, especially since the theory points to how higher levels "transcend and include" lower levels, specifically pointing to how people at lower levels do not see all the dimensions available to people at higher levels. Wilber goes so far as to say

Wilber on Feeling Hungry

"Each person and phenomenon has a subjective, an objective, an intersubjective, and an interobjective aspect. Even the simple process of feeling hungry and planning what to eat (intentional) involves certain brain structures and neurochemistry (behavioral); occurs in a context indicating when, what, and how to eat (cultural); and utilizes some technological means to produce the meal (social)."

Source: Ken Wilber, *The Eye of Spirit: An Integral Vision for a World Gone Slightly Mad.* Boston, Massachusetts: Shambhala Publications, Inc., 1997.

that people at different levels of consciousness live in different worlds. While I have found this tremendously helpful for understanding group dynamics, I have seldom shared this part of Wilber's theory when working in a group. While many might be comfortable acknowledging that a spiritual leader like the Dalai Lama has a higher level of consciousness, few are able to acknowledge a sibling or colleague in the same way.

My first introduction to Wilber's ideas was intriguing enough to inspire further reading. I hope you will keep going too. There are communities of practitioners applying this framework in every field of endeavour, from health and healing, to environment and cities. Perhaps there is a buddy at work who can support you with making Integral Theory a "daily practice." Read on for some suggestions for applying this lens to yourself.

At the personal level

Wilber's Integral Theory aims to map all the dimensions of human consciousness, not just for fun, but to support us to transcend to higher, more embracing, and more beneficial levels of consciousness. First and foremost Integral Theory calls each of us to evolve our consciousness.

I invite you to pause, right this moment, and make a deeper commitment to transforming your consciousness, to your own awakening. You might notice a bit of hesitancy; a fear of the unknown: "Will I be safe?" If this bubbles up, choose to trust. O The part of you that is already whole knows that it is absolutely safe to let go of your current level of consciousness and transcend to the next. Moreover, this territory has been well mapped by those who have gone before as shown by their desire to share the unspeakable benefits!

Those who have gone before have also identified a host of practices that are helpful – everything from yoga and meditation to Tai Chi and contemplative walks in nature. What about you? What helps you to be more present, calm, aware, and awake? Consider making those practices higher priorities in your life. When I feel I do not have time for meditation (my preferred presence practice, yours might be dance!), Integral Theory calls my bluff: those are usually the times when I most need to sit on the cushion!

Integral Theory also calls us to be integral in our journey towards greater consciousness. Most of us have a "quadrant orientation" – one of the quadrants where we feel most at home. For me, it is upper left – the interior individual. Thanks to Integral Theory, I also pay attention to nutrition, exercise, sleep, taking risks (upper right), prioritize practices for questioning cultural values and assumptions (lower left), and build presence practices into how I work with my colleagues and clients (lower right).

What do you already know about the interior and exterior conditions that support you to be more conscious and aware? And how can you have more of these conditions in your life? Perhaps there is one thing you can do today!

It is also helpful to ask, "What is my quadrant orientation?" Take a look at the diagram on page 154, and see which of the four domain descriptions best captures your fundamental stance toward the world. As you do so, invite yourself to open to the other quadrants; value their part in the whole, and perhaps set an intention to bring more of them into your life. Integral Theory is clear that the more we are integral, the more we create conditions for transcending to higher and more joyous levels of being and doing.

Here is one last suggestion: If you have not already done so, take time to map a current challenge in your personal life from the perspective of Integral Theory. Here are prompts to help you tease apart the dynamics of your situation:

- Inspired by the concept of holons, how are you and your challenge nested in wider **wholes**?

- In relation to the challenge, where are you on the spectrum of **self-preservation** and **self-adaptation**? How might you cultivate a dynamic balance of this polarity?

- What comes to light about your situation as you consider different **parts** of yourself? Which of the myriad ways to define yourself are most relevant to your challenge – for example, distinguishing your physical, mental, emotional and spiritual sides, or the different roles you play?

- What new dimensions/elements of your situation can you see thanks to the perspective of each of the **four quadrants** as outlined on page 154? What might you do differently in light of what you now see?

I hope you find this framework as beneficial as I do, and that it supports you to evolve in your own consciousness, and the effectiveness of your work with others.

Links to other chapters

Integral Theory is a map of maps. It teases out dimensions of the other frameworks by inviting us to see them from the perspective of holons, quadrants, levels, and so on. For example, Groundwork's emphasis on our fundamental choice between fear and trust (Interior-Individual) can be made practical by paying attention to the cultural values of the group (Interior-Collective), the way agendas and issues are framed (Exterior-Collective), and our choices about nutrition and rest – since these affect how we show up (Exterior-Individual). Using the quadrants as a checklist can help us engage in ways that raise the level of trust.

Similarly, an Integral approach contributes to a Generative Dialogue and to the Co-Sensing phase in Theory U – through consideration of the quadrants, holons, lines, and levels, etc. Integral Theory also helps us "listen for the whole seeking to emerge" by cultivating greater tolerance for and curiosity about other ways of knowing and being. As you become steeped in Integral Theory, you will become more comfortable with multiple perspectives. This nimbleness helps loosen the hold of your ego, identity, and patterned ways of thinking, and supports breakthroughs to new ways of seeing and doing.

Integral Theory's concept of holons creates a great entry point for Conscious Co-Creation. Noticing holons reveals how life is interconnected webs of wholes that are parts of larger wholes. This perspective can help us expand our awareness to the wider systems of which we are a part. Conscious Co-Creation then gives us insight about how to work in alignment with these larger systems.

The next chapter, on Systemic Constellations, offers complementary perspectives on how parts and wholes are interrelated. From your family of origin, to teams and societal dynamics, its close observation of *what is* has identified three clear principles universally in play when social systems are healthy and harmonious. Read on to gain insight into the hidden dynamics that, once known, can allow us to quickly and profoundly transform our relationships and groups.

Questions

- What more can we see when we consider the wholes that we are part of, and the other parts that make up these wholes?

- Is there a healthy balance in yourself/the group between self-preservation and self-adaptation – between agency and communion?

- Which of the four quadrants are we naturally drawn to, and which do we need to pay more attention to?

- Are we valuing both interior and exterior dimensions and approaches?

- What is our theory of change? Is it Integral – involving all four quadrants?

C

9
Systemic Constellations

"People seek comfort when what they need is courage."
Bert Hellinger

I am in awe of the transformative impact of Systemic Constellations. For starters, it has been of great benefit to me personally. For many years, I struggled with a sense of having both feet on the brakes much as I wanted to go full speed ahead. Then, in a single two-hour session, I gained insight into an unconscious pattern that was holding me in place (I will share more later). After seeing the old pattern, and being helped to see a new healthier pattern, my career took off. Perhaps you can relate to feeling that there is something hidden holding you back in your personal life or career.

Systemic Constellations catalyse this same "unleashing" in other contexts too: our families, groups, teams, initiatives, organizations, companies, networks, and institutions.

I hope what follows encourages you to explore the many ways Systemic Constellations can help you deepen your practice and deepen as a practitioner.

Systemic Constellations

When we look up into the night sky, we see constellations of stars:

recognizable patterns due to the distances and angles between the different (star) elements of, for example, the Big Dipper or The Southern Cross.

Systemic Constellations are similar in that they allow us to see how a person or group understands the distances and angles between different elements of a human system.

In one common form of Systemic Constellations, a person "sets a constellation" to express their gut sense of the inter-relationships in a system. The constellation setter places individual people to "represent" different elements of the system, at specific distances and angles. Who can see whom? Who "has my back", or who is far away? Using our bodies to move representatives into position, not our words, allows our implicit knowing to surface.

Another common form of constellation uses objects on a tabletop to represent system elements, again with placement that feels intuitively right to the person setting the constellation. How we place bodies in space reveals much about how we tacitly understand our situations: the layers deeper than our mental constructs.

Through these simple physical forms, and many others, Systemic Constellations are utilized all over the world in hundreds of applications: from healing intergenerational trauma and helping large corporations with mergers, to prioritizing brand elements in a marketing campaign or exploring character development in "script constellations." MIT's Otto Scharmer uses 4D Mapping, a type of constellation, as a tool for distilling insights from the Co-Sensing phase in his Theory U process.

Constellations work is also fast, as master practitioner Jane Peterson notes, "because it accesses our gut knowing about what's going on rather than winding its way through (the deception of) story.[1]"

It is as if a constellation is a microscope that lets you quickly see previously hidden dimensions of a system. The focus of this chapter, though, is less on the constellations themselves, and

---

1   Source: Email communication from Jane Peterson.

more on what Systemic Constellations have illuminated about the emergent properties[2] of human systems. ⊕

So what are these emergent properties? Here are the four key takeaways that we will unpack in this chapter:

Conscience: rather than being our moral compass, conscience is "a perceptual organ that supports our belonging."

Belonging: humans have a primordial need to belong, and belonging is *the* primary driver of our behaviour.

Give and Take: relationships, groups, and social systems are healthier where there is a balance of giving and receiving.

Social Order: it supports harmony in a human system when everyone knows their place in the social order.

I hope your curiosity is piqued. Before we explore more of this framework, it is important to honour where it has come from.

Origins

The pioneer of Systemic Constellations is Bert Hellinger. Born in 1925, Hellinger grew up in Nazi Germany. Thanks to the influence of his parents' values and faith, he resisted being recruited into the Hilter Youth, and was thereby "Suspected of Being an Enemy of the People". Later conscripted into the German army, he was sent to the Front in 1942, and saw action before being captured and held in a POW camp in Belgium.

A core question emerged from these experiences: "How can good people do bad things with a clear conscience?" In many ways, Hellinger's life work is an answer to this question.

Other significant influences include his 16 years as a Catholic Missionary in Africa. There he was exposed to Zulu language and culture along with the potent, transformative potential of rituals and rites of passage.

---

2 Here is a brief introduction to this important concept: "Living things have different levels of organization. Smaller parts combine to make increasingly complex systems. An emergent property is a characteristic an entity gains when it becomes part of a bigger system. Emergent properties help living organisms better adapt to their environments and increase their chances of survival." Source: Emergent Properties: Definition & Examples http://study.com/academy/lesson/emergent-properties-definition-examples.html

Later, back in Germany, Hellinger trained as psychoanalyst. Key influences on his therapy practice include Virginia Satir's work on family systems and Ivan Boszormenyi-Nagy's descriptions of the hidden bonds and loyalties in families.

Systemic Constellations first emerged in the early 1970s in the group work aspect of Hellinger's practice as a psychoanalyst. There, another key influence was Phenomenology – the practice of seeing with an open mind coupled with systematic reflection to determine the essential properties and patterns of experience.

Hellinger says of his work that for 20 years he was groping in the dark,[3] committed to not imposing his ideas on reality, but rather, in his own words, to "open myself completely to complex connections and allow them to work in me, to affect me."[4]

Thankfully, Hellinger emerged from the darkness, bringing forth concepts that do much to illuminate hidden dynamics in social systems.

Takeaways

In addition to his key insight into conscience, Hellinger discovered what he called the "orders of love", three key patterns that in combination can account for the myriad ways human systems are functional and dysfunctional.

By analogy, to understand flocking in birds, scientists have run simulations with computer programmed "boids" to show that a small number of rules can explain the many ways a flock of birds swoops and dives. The rules allow the boids to fly without hitting or hurting each other.

---

3   Bert Hellinger, *No Waves Without an Ocean*, Heidelberg, Germany: Carl-Auer-Systeme-Verlag, 2006, page 21.

4   Hellinger, Bert, et. al. *Love's Hidden Symmetry: What Makes Love Work in Relationships*. Phoenix, Arizona: Zeig, Tucker and Co., 1998, page 207. Here is another Hellinger quote that gives further insight into the origins of this work: "If I succeed in truly seeing the client, then I'm in contact with something greater than either of us alone. My immediate goal can't even be to help, but only to see the client in the context of a larger order. That's how seeing works, and it allows therapeutic interventions to remain respectful and loving, while at the same time being a force for healing." Source: ibid., page 206.

Similarly, following the patterns Hellinger identified allows us to be in right relationship with each other in our social systems.

Let's unpack the four key insights coming from Systemic Constellations, starting with Belonging.

Belonging

Humans are social creatures, and belonging – being part of a group – is a biological imperative for our survival.

For each of us, our first and most important group is our family of origin, or the FOO Factor as Jane Peterson affectionately calls it. As a small dependent child, each of us did whatever it took to belong to our family, most of us being exquisitely wired to read faces and gestures, along with tone of voice and body language. (An exception might be people on the autism spectrum, which helps to account for their challenges with connecting to other people.)

We learn from our families of origin what it takes to belong in that context. This learning is typically implicit rather than explicit: we have a gut feeling that guides us rather than a conscious thought or decision. Then we unconsciously carry forward these body-based "maxims" into other contexts in the rest of our life, where these same maxims often get in our way.

My FOO story

In my case, as a small child, I sensed my father's need for mothering (his mother died when he was 8), and did my best to fill that gap. This meant that my life energy was oriented "upstream" and tied up in rescuing my father as a way to make it safe for me. As a result, I did not have energy for being a leader in my own life, and unconsciously created patterns of my true life's work being beyond my reach. See Image #1 showing how I placed different elements in a tabletop constellation.

In Image #2, you can see a very different picture: I have the blessing of my father "at my back", and my work and clients are within reach. For weeks after the session, I carried Image #2 around in my wallet and kept it visible by my desk. I was integrating a new "constellation" of the primary elements in my life, shifting to a new understanding of how I belonged in my family. Three weeks after that constellation, I got a call out of the blue that launched a new and much more potent chapter of my work. I was ready to accept that challenge, whereas before I might have been hesitant.

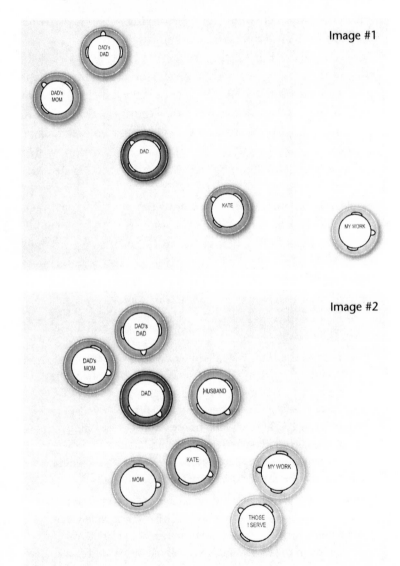

Image #1

Image #2

Belonging is always context dependent. We behave differently in different groups, doing one thing when out with the guys/gals, and behaving very differently at tea with a great aunt. Or one thing at work and perhaps the opposite at home.

Seeing this need to belong played out over and over led Hellinger to his understanding of conscience.

Conscience

One of Hellinger's great contributions is to distinguish conscience from morality and the associated concepts of good and evil. This is a radical departure: in our typical understanding, "conscience" refers to the inner feeling or voice that helps us discern right from wrong and to act in a moral way.

As noted earlier, Hellinger was struck by how good people can do bad things with a clear conscience. Yes, conscience guides us, but "the only criteria followed by conscience ... are the values of the group to which we belong."[5] Or as Jane Peterson puts it, "Conscience isn't about doing the right thing, it's about belonging. Conscience is this early, implicit learning of how to behave so we are included in our groups."[6]

Belonging for change

Perhaps you have heard the expression, "The quickest way to change yourself is to change the company you keep." If you want to change behaviour, one powerful strategy is to create a group that people can belong to that has this new behaviour at its core. Take Alcoholics Anonymous, Lawyers for Social Responsibility, or the excellent Dreamrider initiative that invites kids to become "Planet Protectors."

I hope you will take a moment to reflect on the implications of this different definition of conscience. It may challenge how you think things should be, but I suspect it will better illuminate how things actually are. For example, if you frame your work as being

---

5   Ibid., page 9.

6   Source: Email communication from Jane Peterson.

against "them" who do bad things, know "they" likely act with a good conscience, and that individuals within "they" are bonded to their group, just as you are bonded to yours. This is how people can, in good conscience, be suicide bombers and terrorists, gang members and robbers.

This is also not the whole story. By conscious effort, individuals can "leave behind what we have known and follow the Conscience of the Greater Whole." Then, when cut lose from belonging to a specific group, we have to feel our way forward.[7] ↺

Give and Take

Our need to belong has a corollary in our need to serve the interests of the groups we belong to. As a result, our conscience is finely tuned to what helps create a good flow of energy and good outcomes in our groups. After belonging, the final two "orders of love" that Hellinger names are patterns he found to be in play when there is wellbeing and vitality in social groups. The first of these is Give and Take.

Hellinger discerned that love flows in families when there is a dynamic balancing of give and take that he calls "full exchange". For example, out of love, the wife gives to the husband. The husband receives with gratitude, and gives back to the wife, giving a little bit more than the wife gave. In turn the wife gives again to the husband, matching and slightly exceeding what he gave, and so on. The bond between the husband and wife grows over time thanks to their active participation in successive waves of generous giving and receiving. Meanwhile, children receive from their parents without fully giving back to them while children, and balance give and take by later giving, in turn, to their children, to their aging parents, or to the wider world.

We also often balance give and take by "fasting" and "helping". I see both these sub-patterns in myself. When I am "fasting", I cut myself off from contact with others and do not ask for or receive

---

7   Hellinger, Bert, et. al. *Love's Hidden Symmetry: What Makes Love Work in Relationships.* Phoenix, Arizona: Zeig, Tucker and Co., 1998, page 4.

help. This keeps me free from feeling obligated to help to others: I do not have to balance give and take if I do not receive at all. However, not participating in give and take with others also isolates me and cuts me off from the richness that comes from the diverse perspectives, skills, energy, kindness, and love others can give me. The pandemic of loneliness in Western culture has much to do with such "fasting".

When I am acting out of the "helping" dynamic, I give and give to others generously until I feel entitled to receive (and righteously resentful if others do not give back to me.) This over-emphasis on giving keeps me from having to experience the vulnerability of my need for others' love and support.

Do you see yourself and others in these patterns? Doing so can help us shift to Hellinger's full exchange, the approach that nurtures the groups and relationships that in turn nurture us.

As you look for these patterns, you will see that they show up in all sorts of ways. For example, at one point, I thought how wonderful it would be if the Dalai Lama endorsed this book, but at first felt I could not ask. "Why?", I wondered. It felt like taking too much. When I later realized that I was asking in service of being able to help readers and their work to help others (something I believe the Dalai Lama cares about), I was then able to ask.

Our felt sense (conscience) lets us know when we are out of balance with giving and receiving. This is a good thing. It helps us be in right relationship in the social groups we are part of. I suspect your lived experience is like mine: social systems thrive when there are rich networks of giving and receiving.

Social Order

Social systems also thrive where social order is respected.

This general pattern plays out in many ways, depending on the context, but generally speaking there are two main ingredients: those who come first go first (rank higher), as do those who contribute the most to meeting the survival needs of the group.

For example, parents come before children, as they are able to create more children in service of continuing the social group, while children are too young to reproduce, and are dependant on parents to survive.

This is another pattern often unconsciously flouted. For example, a constellation once helped me see my relationship with the boss and founder of a company I worked for: I set a constellation to gain insight into why I felt unable to contribute as fully as I wanted to at work. I placed myself in front of and quite close to my boss, looking "upstream", and between my boss and the company's clients. If you notice a similarity with my family of origin, you are not wrong. I was out of social order, contesting the boss's leadership. Once I saw the option of being beside my boss, and both looking together to meet the needs of our clients, I felt much more harmony. By shifting internally to be "in the right place", I was more comfortable in my skin. Ironically, by letting go of asserting myself, I was subsequently more confident, and more able to contribute as I had wanted to.

Here are two more stories of how the "orders of love" support life energy to flow in social systems. First, though, it will be helpful to share one more bit about Systemic Constellations: if people setting a constellation with representatives do so authentically, "the representatives begin to have feelings and thoughts very close to those the [system] members felt – *without prior knowledge.*"[8] Read on to see an example of how this unfolds in practice.

Systemic Constellations in action

In a workshop, a Chinese venture capitalist (VC) set a constellation. His business was based on buying companies in trouble, turning them around, and selling them at a profit. He had been doing this for years with much success, but had recently purchased a machinery business where his usual formula was not working. Despite addressing many glaring issues in the systems and procedures of the company, sales kept falling. The VC was looking for insights into how to move forward. He was very frustrated with the founders of the company, and aggressively blamed them as the source of the problems.

---

8   Ibid., page xii.

The VC was invited to choose representatives for his firm, the founders (who remained in the management team), the clients, and the VC staff members.

Once the constellation was underway, the felt sense of the client representatives was a desire to leave the constellation and lay down (making visible the dynamics underlying the falling sales). As the client representatives left the constellation, the representative for the founders broke into tears, clearly in great distress. The VC staff representatives flanked the founders, glaring at them, but the founders only had eyes for the client. The client was repelled by the tension.

This was a turning point. Up until then, the VC had wanted to get rid of the founders – to push them out of the picture. When asked, the founders' representative expressed love and respect for their clients and deep desire to serve them well. This triggered a big "Aha" for the VC: the founders *loved* their clients. The business was about much more than the bottom line for the founders. They truly cared about their clients and had formed strong bonds with them. Hearing the founders' love, the clients' rep stirred, stood up, and rejoined the system.

This gave the VC a deep appreciation for why the founders had created the company in the first place, an insight that touched the VC deeply, almost moving him to tears. The insight also completely changed how the VC saw the founders. He shifted from derision for their business mistakes (misreading the market and poor investment decisions) to respect for the depth of their caring and the strength of the bonds they had formed with customers. And with this, he knew his way forward: not pushing the founders out, but honouring them and what they had created, and building on their deep feeling for their clients.

In terms of the patterns Hellinger identified, this story points to the importance of social order: honouring those who came first – in this case the founders, and their relationship with their clients. Without them, there would have been no business opportunity for the VC to capitalize on.

The pattern revealed in this story also applies in non-profit organizations, social movements, and networks. Too often people passionate to make a difference fail to honour the work and ground gained by those who have come before. Simple heart-felt actions to acknowledge the lineage of your work can have significant impact on how things unfold. I hope you will do your own experiments.

Here is an example of a quick diagnostic constellation that allows a system to see itself, and thereby address gaps. △

Four Functions

Jane Peterson was working with a business-to-business company, one that provides services to clients that are businesses. Jane named four functions, and, creating a diamond pattern, assigned an area in the room to each one: Governance, Operations, Finance & Legal, and Sales & Marketing. Then she invited the 20 people at the meeting to reflect in silence on where they felt they brought the most value to the company in terms of those four options. The next step was to ask people to move to the part of the diamond that represented their greatest contribution to the company.

A clear pattern quickly emerged: most of the people were clustered in Sales & Marketing with one or two in Finance & Legal. No one was holding the Governance function (the CEO was in Sales & Marketing), and there was one lonely person in Operations.

To thrive, a business, non-profit, or institution needs all four functions to be performed. This 20-minute activity allowed the company to see the significant gap they had in Governance. While the CEO was very resistant to taking his rightful (social order) place in Governance, his ultimate decision to do so enabled others to do their jobs freely.

I hope these stories whet your appetite for the possibilities of applying the insights of the Systemic Constellations framework, and perhaps even some of its processes for working with groups. Either way, here are finer points and possible pitfalls to consider.

Finer points

- Belonging, Give and Take, and Social Order are emergent properties of human systems, meaning that they are context dependent. It is important not to turn Hellinger's insights into overly simplistic, or hard and fast rules. Remember that the source of these patterns was Hellinger seeing what brought greater ease and harmony for his clients. It is important to stay rooted in people's felt sense of what nourishes harmony and helps love to flow, rather than in abstract concepts of what should be. This means that while we can definitely learn from the patterns, we should hold them lightly and remain curious about the specifics of each context and system.

- In delving deeper into context dependence, it can be helpful to distinguish between biological and social systems. See the table below for how Jane Peterson elaborates. Hold this lightly too.

Orders of Love & Orders of Relationship

	Family	Organization	
Biological, Emergent System	**BELONGING**		**Socially Constructed System**
	• All members belong	• Belonging is contingent on performance relative to organizational purpose	
	GIVE & TAKE		
	• Reinforce and strengthen bonds between members • Increase resiliency of the system	• Equal to contribution • Enable members to separate and move to other groups as both need	
	SOCIAL ORDER		
	• First in in first place • New systems take priority over older ones (fission)	Competing goals: • First in in first place • Those who contribute must be acknowledged • Those who make it possible are first	

For example, I am currently in an inquiry about how to apply this table to social networks. I suspect that they are more like biological systems than social systems.

- We generally sense social order in a team, organization, company, or country as a weighted basket of two main factors: who came first, and how well each contributes to the purpose of the entity. Thus we enshrine seniority in our personnel policies and our pay scales typically give greater rewards to those who make more unique or essential contributions. Since seniority is easier to measure, many social systems overly weight their HR practices to this measure. A new person who brings skills or perspectives sorely needed at a particular juncture is too often sidelined by strict adherence to seniority-based practices. Both contributions must be honoured.

- The history of a system affects the system. This is perhaps too obvious to bother stating. At the same time, over and over I see in my work that people neglect finding about what has gone before in the systems they join or want to influence. For example, have there been past betrayals? Has give and take been balanced over time? Has the social order been respected? As just one example, these questions applied to indigenous peoples' relationships with settler populations will help you to orient much better to the dynamics of the situation.

- If you cannot quite put your finger on the dynamics of a human system, one helpful question coming from this framework is to ask, "Whose needs are being served?" Seemingly paradoxical actions make sense once you understand hidden loyalties and drivers. You are more likely to suss out the dynamics if you ask, "Who is benefiting?"

- Like the story of the four functions, it can be very helpful to a group to make visible the allocations and interrelationships between different elements. One classic activity is asking group members to line up in order of who came first. It is not unusual for us to have some ideas about founders and those who joined close to when we did, but little idea of who came when at other times. This helps people to know *that* they belong and

SYSTEMIC CONSTELLATIONS

HUMAN SYSTEMS THRIVE WHEN THEY
FOLLOW THE THREE ORDERS OF LOVE:

BELONGING – EVERYONE IN A FAMILY BELONGS

GIVE AND TAKE – BALANCE GIVE AND TAKE OVER TIME

SOCIAL ORDER – HONOUR THOSE WHO CAME BEFORE US

where they belong, and to honour those who have come before. Remember to temper this with awareness of the contributions different people bring.

Possible pitfalls

- One of the most common pitfalls I now observe as a result of working with Systemic Constellations is the failure to honour founders and leaders who have gone before. Something as simple as putting up a beautiful photograph of the founder, when done with sincere respect, can be enough to unleash a flood of positive energy in a system.

- It can cause problems if you create overly rigid definitions of social order in a system. For example, self-managed organizations function best when leadership (high rank) moves around the group, to the person(s) who have most to contribute depending on the tasks and issues at hand: for example, people learn to go to Cynthia for task management and to Rajiv for communications.

- In order for love and goodwill to flow and trust to be established, hurts need to be repaired without causing more damage to the system. If the "victim" asks for recompense, but not revenge, the system will be restored to balance and the "aggressor" can remain part of the system without endangering the coherence of the system.

The above finer points and possible pitfalls are the top tips out of hundreds of possible considerations. I truly hope you will delve deeper into the potential of this framework. It is on my cutting edge, and I believe that its access to body wisdom and to systemic dimensions make it more important now than ever before.

At the personal level

As always, an important way to deepen your understanding of a framework is to apply it to yourself. Here are key suggestions:
- Our early experiences in our family of origin have tremendous unconscious influence on how we behave in all sorts of

situations. Systemic Constellations is a very powerful approach to gaining insight into the hidden loyalties and agreements originating in our family that are unconsciously running our lives. Based on my own experience, I strongly recommend finding a constellations practitioner in your area and setting a personal constellation. If you do so, you may well find that dysfunctional patterns in your work context shift almost miraculously – for example, bosses who do not value your contribution, or always feeling on the outside of the team.

- Whether or not you do your own FOO constellation, one of the most important relationships in your life is the one you have with your parents. There, this simple fact is the most fundamental: without my parents, I would not be here. If you, like me, have wanted something more or different from a parent or your parents, then you will likely experience a surge in well-being and agency if you shift from entitlement to gratitude, and from resentment to acceptance.

- Reflect on your life from the perspective of belonging. If you feel you do not belong, get curious. It may be that you are out of social order: overstepping your place and so feeling you do not belong. It may be that you are withholding what you can contribute, for fear of being rejected – a counterproductive strategy that actually undermines your right to belong in that social system.

- It is also helpful to reflect on how you navigate give and take. Do you tend to "fast", as I do, cutting myself off from others so that I do not have any obligations to give back? Or you might be a helper. Either way, flex the muscles of full exchange in your relationships, the better to support greater vitality and resilience in your social relations.

Links to other chapters

The Systemic Constellation framework is about how to have more energy and love flowing in human systems. As such, it touches on every other framework in the book. Here are a few specifics:

- To sharpen Groundwork's attention to trust, add in reflections on belonging, give and take, and social order. Where people are in right relationship, trust is a natural corollary.

- Systemic Constellations, Process Work, Theory U, and Conscious Co-Creation all share concepts of the *field*. Being more fluent with these non-visible elements of human systems is a powerful way to become better at navigating complex dynamics.

- Process Work and Systemic Constellations both speak about rank and social order. Process Work does it from the point of view of Deep Democracy, calling us to embrace a system's disturbing secondary process to have more inclusive health and vitality. At a superficial level, Systemic Constellations work appears more focused on the status quo – bringing a system into greater harmony as defined by how it sets the boundaries of caring. Both frameworks add insights. Both are important. I hope you use each to challenge and enrich the insights of the other.

- Integral Theory calls us to consider our situation from all four quadrants, including collective as well as individual dimensions. Systems Constellations is focused on inter-relationships between different elements of a system. They are both systemic, and both challenge Western culture's excessive emphasis on the individual as a unit of analysis.

- Systemic Constellations includes an understanding of "Conscience of the Greater Whole". If you are inspired to dig deeper into this aspect, I suspect you will find overlap with the next and final framework in this book, Conscious Co-Creation.

Questions

- How is our human need to belong playing out in this context?
- Is there a good balance of give and take in this context?
- Is social order being acknowledged, for example, by honouring founders or those who have been working in this field before us?
- What history in this context needs to be acknowledged?
- Who is benefiting from the status quo?

10
Conscious Co-Creation

*You are the outer extension of ourselves
as we are the inner extensions of you.
Let the oneness grow in your awareness.*

The Devas[1]

Conscious Co-Creation burst into my world on April 21, 1990, the day I arrived at the Findhorn Foundation, an educational center and intentional community in Northern Scotland.

Conscious Co-Creation's greatest gift to me has been weaving love into the fabric of my life, gradually displacing fear, righteousness, and judgment of myself and others. It has been like a steady course correction, bringing me ever more into alignment with who I really am and what is most alive.

Working co-creatively is effective and joyous, and has been particularly potent for my work in groups. Instead of struggling as a lone wolf, I am supported and inspired, and there are more synergies and synchronicities; more dynamism and sweetness.

It is a great pleasure to share this lens with you, one that invites

---

1 The Findhorn Community. *The Findhorn Garden: Pioneering a New Vision of Humanity and Nature in Cooperation* (Second Edition). Forres, Scotland: Findhorn Press, 1975, page 80.

us to work consciously and collaboratively with the intelligent life force that infuses everything, everywhere and always. ↺ C

Origins

In 1962, despite their best efforts to find work, Peter and Eileen Caddy and Dorothy McLean were living on social assistance in a caravan park a few miles outside Findhorn village. Each of them was highly functional and high-powered, and together they pursued a rigorous path of spiritual growth including meditation, reflection, and an ironclad commitment to acting on intuition.

Living with Peter, Eileen, and Dorothy were the Caddy's three teenaged sons. Feeding six people on social assistance was challenging. To make ends meet, Peter created a vegetable garden next to their tiny trailer.

In May 1963, while she was meditating, Dorothy received an insight calling her to connect with the forces of nature. Hearing of her insight, Peter suggested that she help with the garden.

Dorothy connected first with one of her favourite vegetables, the garden pea – sitting in meditation and inviting contact on the inner. She soon realized that she was communicating, not with a specific plant, but with the "overlighting being," or essence[2] of the species: "the consciousness holding the archetypal design of the species and the blueprint for its highest potential."[3]

Thanks to instructions received by "tuning in" to the essence of each species, the vegetables and flowers in the garden soon grew to legendary proportions – 40-pound cabbages and eight-foot delphiniums.

Through her daily meditations, Dorothy received precise instructions from the carrot essence, for example, as to watering, mulching, thinning, etc. for carrot seedlings. Along with the

---

2 Dorothy called the overlighting essences "devas." "Deva" is a Sanskrit word meaning "shining one." The closest English translation is "angel." Dorothy preferred the word "deva" though even it was not quite right. Angel had too much form (wings, long gowns, wands ...). What Dorothy experienced was a specific, non-visible, beneficial force.

3 Findhorn Foundation website, quoted with permission – http://www.findhorn.org/aboutus/vision/co-creation

specific gardening instructions, the essence gave more general insights about the importance of love, and how to work co-creatively (see sidebar, Sample deva messages).

Sample deva messages to Dorothy[4]

We see life in terms of the inner force while you see only the outer form and cannot see the continual process taking place. We should like you to try to think in our terms, because it will make things easier for both of us – you will be closer to reality and will also be able to understand us better.

♦♦♦

You are in the world of action where we are not physically embodied, and that is your great opportunity and privilege. You are the outer extension of ourselves as we are the inner extensions of you. Let the oneness grow in your awareness.

♦♦♦

Just tune into nature until you feel the love flow.... Always it is your state that the nature world responds to, not what you say, not what you do, but what you are.

During the early years, the garden attracted attention from soil experts and horticulturalists stunned by the inexplicable size of the vegetables and flowers. This put the community on the map, and attracted hundreds of people to join the experiment and thousands more as short-term visitors. Adapting the lessons learned from the garden has been integral to the community's success in all its other dimensions.

The Foundation has grown and diversified steadily, and today is the nucleus of a thriving spiritual community and "ecovillage," the birthplace of dozens of global initiatives, and the hub of a vibrant international network of individuals and organizations.

You do not need to subscribe to Dorothy's worldview to benefit from Conscious Co-Creation. You simply need to be open to

---

4 The Findhorn Community. *The Findhorn Garden: Pioneering a New Vision of Humanity and Nature in Cooperation* (Second Edition). Forres, Scotland: Findhorn Press, 1975, pages 79 and 81.

experimenting and seeing where it takes you. Here is more of what I learned about Conscious Co-Creation while I was at the Findhorn Foundation.

Conscious Co-Creation with nature

Conscious Co-Creation invites us to nurture an intentional partnership between humans and nature. Instead of seeing nature (including ourselves and others) as something to be conquered, this lens invites us to see all of life as interconnected, sacred, and intelligent. It invites us to pay attention to the life force in everything, and to notice that just as a child responds to love, so does *everything* else.

Conscious Co-Creation means collaborating with this non-visible dimension, however we understand it, by acknowledging its presence, asking it for help, and then being open to indications of what will serve the highest for all concerned. ∧ Doing so brings human activity into greater harmony with nature. ○

The partnership is like walking – a seamless integration of two sides, moving us forward. As humans, we bring our hands, heads, and hearts – including all our skills, knowledge, and the benefits of past experience. The overlighting essence brings insights and guidance ranging from big picture thinking to very specific instructions.

Working co-creatively is like having an "X Factor" backing you up. You can create the human systems equivalent of 40-pound cabbages: outstanding results achieved with grace, ease, and joy. The right people show up at the right time. Different elements click. Actions, results, and possibilities shift up to the next level.

How to work co-creatively

To be able to work in partnership with life, start by doing Groundwork as described on page 13, or lay a foundation in your own way. Such initial preparation is essential, since it brings you into alignment with your essence, and therefore into harmony with life.

Once we have prepared our inner "ground," working co-creatively involves these three steps.

1. Ask for help.

2. Find ways to listen.

3. Honour the insights, perspectives, and suggestions received.

You can do these steps on your own, or as a group. For example, you can work on your own to connect with the energetic essence of a group or organization you are part of. In addition, groups of people can adapt an individual-based process to a group context.

1. *Ask for help.*

Asking for help requires openness to the possibility of non-visible support for your work. You do not need to be convinced that there is an essence for your project. It is enough to be open to the possibility. Asking for help can be as simple as saying or thinking something like: "To the essence of, for example, the Literacy Project, please help things unfold in the best possible ways."

Inviting help in this way is profound. Most of us are almost addicted to struggle. Westerners, in particular, have a strong independent streak. It takes humility and openness to welcome assistance, perhaps because doing so starts a change process, and most of us are ambivalent about change, even when it is for the better!

2. *Find ways to listen.*

Having asked for help, listen to how life responds. The odds are excellent that you already have had your own experiences of intuitive knowing – perhaps a gut instinct about a person, a penchant for noticing synchronicities when you have an urgent question, or an intuitive flash about an opportunity. Reflecting on these experiences will help you know how messages come to you, and whether you typically listen to or dismiss their wisdom.

Some people pay attention to their body sensations. Others do an inner work practice, such as automatic writing or guided visualization. Many of us listen to "flirts" – a sign or signal that catches our attention, such as something said by a friend, or words on a billboard. For step-by-step introductions to flirts, inner guides and other ways to access inner knowing, see my first book *Make Light Work: 10 Tools for Inner Knowing.*[5]

3. *Honour the insights, perspectives, and suggestions received.*

The third and final step is to honour the contributions of the overlighting essence. Treat the input with respect. Respond to it authentically. If you have reservations, articulate them, and be open to continuing the dialogue, as the essence may have further insights and options. If the recommendations ring true, put them into effect. If you are not ready to take such a leap, articulate why. No matter what, give thanks for the contributions. In this way, you will cultivate a stronger and deeper relationship with the essence for your project/organization/etc.

It is truly as simple as this. It is as if you are asking for help from the wisest person you know. Approaching them involves opening yourself to seeing things differently. You listen with an open heart, and an open mind, and an open will. You value the input and consider it carefully and respectfully. You let it touch you and affect how you act. And you give thanks! Over time, you develop a relationship, which like any other relationship becomes more intimate and rich the more we open our hearts and bring our authentic selves to the table.

◆◆◆

Each of us needs to find our own way to connect with life to work co-creatively. The story below recounts one person's first experience of co-creative communication. Mainstream society does not value such moments. We have to go against a strong current to value them ourselves, as sensing the oneness of all of life does not

5   Sutherland, Kate. *Make Light Work: 10 Tools for Inner Knowing.* Vancouver, British Columbia: Incite Press, 2010.

fit with our emphasis on rational, logical, and scientific ways of knowing, or the programs and structures of Western society.

Conscious Co-Creation in action[6]

Alan Watson heard of the Findhorn Foundation through a book. He found a copy of *The Findhorn Garden* in a bookstore in New York City in early 1978, read it cover to cover in three days, and knew that he would visit the community when he got back to Scotland a month later.

Alan was at a turning point in his life. Working for environmental groups had been like "putting a plaster over a major wound instead of treating the cause of the injury." He sought clarity about how best to contribute to making the world a better place.

After a two-week visit, Alan went to live at the Findhorn Foundation in the fall of 1978. A few months later, he became responsible for the vegetable garden at the Foundation's Cluny Hill College, despite having no previous experience growing vegetables. Dorothy had left the community several years earlier, and others from the early days were either dead or not sharing what they knew about working co-creatively with nature.

Left to his own devices, Alan "had to turn to the garden itself – to the plants, animals, and the spirit there – to find what [he] needed in order to do [his] work." He adds, "I started by spending a lot of time just looking at what was in the garden and seeing how things began to grow as spring commenced." He also drew on his first experiences of being fully responsible for houseplants – thanks to having several in his room at Findhorn: "I found that the amount of love I gave them had a very real and visible effect on them. I started to apply this principle to the garden and as time went by I developed a sense of attunement with the vegetables such that most of the time it was obvious to me what they needed."

Alan also noticed that the vegetables he liked to eat did better than the ones he did not, even though he gave both categories

---

6   The Findhorn Community. *The Findhorn Garden: Pioneering a New Vision of Humanity and Nature in Cooperation* (Second Edition). Forres, Scotland: Findhorn Press, 1975, pages 179-183. Story condensed with permission.

the water they needed and good amounts of compost. "What I was learning was that the way in which I did my work, and specifically how much love I could do it with, was at least as important as the work itself."

With time, Alan also had a profound experience of the oneness of life. Here is how he tells the story, taking time to set up the context so you can have a vivid picture of the breakthrough he experienced:

"I was looking after a group of guests ... for an afternoon. They were planting out leeks in the vegetable garden, which takes the form of several concentric circles. The entire circular area is divided into four quadrants, each of which is planted with a different type of vegetable crop. ... The type of crop in each quadrant then changes each year through a rotational system so that soil fertility is maintained.

While the guests planted leeks in the leaf vegetable quadrant, I got on with my own work, digging cooked food scraps into a trench just outside the circular area so that they would compost underground without smelling and attracting rats. I had been working away at this for some time when some flies started buzzing around me. I ignored them at first, thinking they had been attracted by the food scraps. However, after a while I noticed that they weren't flying around the scraps, but around my head. I remembered what i had been told about insect pests – that they are part of the whole and should receive human love instead of our disgust and mistreatment. Closing my eyes for a few moments I tried to open my heart and accept the flies as part of the whole, while at the same time asking them to leave me alone. But when I opened my eyes they were still buzzing around me.

A few minutes later one of the flies landed on my face, right in the corner of my eye. In the course of brushing it away I looked up ... and noticed the guests planting the leeks. I had been so fully engaged in my own work that I had forgotten them. ... I saw that the woman who had been planting the innermost circle ... had finished the quadrant where the leeks were supposed to be and had moved on to the second and third quadrants … I had to go over and tell her to take them out so that they could be replanted in the outermost circle of the first quadrant.

After acknowledging her feelings about undoing her lovingly done work of the last half hour or so, I went back to my own work. It was only after several minutes that I realized the flies were gone, and when I did so I stopped digging, because I knew that something significant had just taken place. The flies had not been buzzing me by chance. There had been a purpose to it, which was to draw me out of my private space and see what was happening around me. When I hadn't got the message, one of the flies landed in the corner of my eye as a clear sign that I should use my eyes.

This was an important moment for me. I knew that I had experienced my own contact with the spirit of nature – a very down-to-earth, practical one. I don't have any rational explanation for what occurred, whether the deva of the leeks was communicating with me through the flies or whatever. For me that is not important. What is significant is that this experience demonstrated to me in very real terms the fact of the oneness of all life."

As you reflect on Alan's story, I suspect you will recall your own experiences of connectedness, perhaps thanks to synchronicities you cannot explain, or to being in a place in nature that opens your heart in a special way. Your experience might not sound like much to another person, but you *know* without question that you experienced an important connection to life. This awareness will give you a touchstone for the texture of such moments.

When we ask for help from the overlighting essence of our company, project, initiative, etc., it may be that the message comes in the form of a subtle signal, such as Alan's buzzing flies.

Attunement

We can tap more of the potential of Conscious Co-Creation by using different forms of "attunement." At the Findhorn Foundation, attunement is used for making decisions of all types, and for helping groups of people come into harmony for everything from doing simple tasks to setting strategic directions. ↻

How? The first step is to do personal Groundwork of some sort (see page 13). With this base, the second step, again for you personally, is to "tune into," as in consciously connect with, the overlighting essence of the group or project.

In many instances, this is as far as you need to go. Simply attuning yourself to the essence of an initiative brings you into alignment such that you are more likely to speak and act in ways that are in harmony with life. If you have "tuned" the instrument of yourself to be in harmony with the overlighting energy in your situation, then you will make beautiful music.

You can amplify the impact of an attunement in a group context by involving others.

Musical metaphors

Notice the musical terms: harmony, resonance, and being in tune. When people in a choir sing in harmony, it is powerful and pleasing. Everyone is "singing from the same song sheet," and the counterpoint of different voices creates a beautiful resonance.

Inviting group members to "attune to" the essence of their group, or to connect to a strong sense of shared purpose ☉, is a powerful way to come into harmony/alignment. As with the musical metaphor, there is space for the uniqueness of each voice (person), and there is a melding of the different contributions that is greater than the sum of the parts.

You do not have to call it an attunement, and people do not have to know what you are doing. For example, Evan Renaerts has brought the practice of attunement to industrial construction job sites when he oversees short-term repair shutdowns. While giving an orientation to a job crew, he never speaks of overlighting essences. He does, however, speak from a place of his own inner connection to the essence of the job, and he talks about such shared purposes as having a safe shutdown, and this project as one of those sweet jobs that everyone still talks about years later.

If your group is open to the idea of attuning to an overlighting essence, or whatever words work in your context, you can quickly create an unusually high level of harmony and alignment with purpose ☉ in the group. To do so, start by doing Groundwork yourself. Then connect personally with the overlighting essence for your group. Once you feel "attuned," invite others to do some form of Groundwork and make their own personal connection with the overlighting essence.

As an example of what to say, see the Sample Group Attunement sidebar. It shares how Brita Atkinson, a former member of the Findhorn Foundation, opened a meeting intended to bridge the divide between mainstream medical doctors and alternative health practitioners. Notice the overall structure of (1) naming shared purpose, (2) inviting group members to center and ground, and (3) inviting specific qualities, such as open-heartedness and appreciativeness.

Group decision-making

Going further, groups can attune to an overlighting essence to help with making decisions and setting direction. A typical process at the Findhorn Foundation uses inner work tools such as meditation or guided visualization to seek guiding images, insights, and perspectives from within.

One common practice is to visualize the essence of a group, project, or task as something easy to imagine – a pool of water, a ball of light, or a flower such as a rose. How does the image change when presented with different options? For example, does the rose blossom, brighten, wither, or change colour? There are as many visualization images and approaches as there are creative people. The key is to (1) ask for help, (2) find a way to listen, and (3) honour what you receive.

Through such inner work practices, group members receive precise information as practical, relevant, and effective as the instructions from the carrot essence for watering. Decisions are often unanimous, even where previously there was conflict or fundamental disagreement. (See Coda, page 213, for one example.)

Sample Group Attunement

"We are gathering here today to reach out to one another and share our skills, expertise, insights, and knowledge. The purpose of our meetings is to expand our awareness of how the human body becomes sick or out of balance, and learn more about all the methods healthcare practitioners can use to assist people in their path to recovery. We appreciate that there are many different methods and modalities available in the Bellingham and Whatcom County area.

"Now let us take a moment to still our minds. Please sit comfortably and relax your body as much as you can. Please, for a few moments, close or half-close your eyes and come to a state of peace and stillness. Let us take a few deep breaths. (Pause.) Now, become aware of your own inner essence, your soul – your deepest aspect of awareness. Appreciate yourself for taking time to come to this meeting. Now, bring into your awareness all the other people in this room and appreciate them also for taking time to come here to share knowledge and help increase one another's awareness in different ways. Allow your heart to open. We envision that all of us open our hearts in an atmosphere of caring and support. (Pause.)

"Now let us ask that this meeting today and all upcoming meetings will be held in this atmosphere of openness and sharing, and let us be thankful for all the new information and insights we are giving and receiving. Thank you.

"When you are ready, open your eyes again."

Attunement is quicker and more effective than traditional consensus-building. Where consensus decision-making often bogs down due to personal histories and agendas, attunement brings out the best in us by cutting through the personality level to where there is unity of purpose based on alignment with life.

Here are two anecdotes from Brita that give practical examples of working with attunement for making decisions and gaining insights.

Attunement in action – youth group

One time, in the Findhorn Foundation, we in the education management committee needed to make a decision about a proposal. The youth group in our local community had approached us requesting a loan of £30,000 to erect a small building to be a gathering place for young people to have weekly meetings, classes, and workshops.

After due discussion, eight of us sat quietly in a circle and one person led an attunement. We tuned in to the overlighting being of the Findhorn Foundation and asked if it would be the right step forward to grant the youth group the loan they requested. After a few minutes of silence, we opened our eyes and each committee member shared their insights.

To our surprise, most of us had received a whole new perspective on the issue in our silence. Six of us, including me, said we felt we should not go ahead and loan the amount to the youth group, and instead we should simply donate the amount to them. Two people had different insights. One said we should not provide the money, the other said we should offer them the loan they requested. The two people who had a different view agreed to go ahead with the decision most of us wanted. Thus, a decision was made to donate £30,000.

The youth group was stunned and overjoyed when we told them. Within a few months, the new building was constructed and it was received with great energy and excitement.

If we had not had the silent attunement, I, for one, would not have had the insight to give away the money rather than loan it to the group, and I believe none of us would have thought of it.

This story demonstrates how attunement brought options to the table that had not been considered by any of the people in the system. Interestingly, there was far more support for a normally marginalized group – the youth – than would otherwise have occurred. ∧

Brita's second story shows how an individual, alone and at any time, can attune to the essence of a group or project or organization.

Attunement in action – Lions Club

I have been a member of our local Lions Club for a few years.
I enjoy the interaction with others who live nearby, and it is a
way for me to stay connected to the local community. The club
organizes a yearly Easter egg hunt; assists people on low incomes
who need new glasses, a wheelchair, or the like; and offers a free
breakfast at our local school every spring as a way to celebrate
our community. However, on occasion I think the entire Lions
Club movement needs to change with the times. For example,
I wish we would use more organic ingredients when we do
catering and improve our recycling systems.

Recently I asked the overlighting essence of the Lions Club: "Hey,
what can I do to facilitate change? I don't really know how to
go about it." Immediately, I had an answer, but different from
what I expected: "Brita, you do not have to do anything. You are
already doing a lot to help others and have done it all your life.
It is not what you need to do right now. You need to turn that
joy to serve into serving your own needs at this point. Trust that
the changes you like to see will be taking place in the course of
time."

This story shows how simply and quickly one can gain important insights through tuning into an overlighting essence. I hope
it inspires you to experiment, and that you find a way to attune
that works for you.

Here are finer points and possible pitfalls for working
co-creatively.

Finer points

- A great way to get started is to experiment. For example, pick
  one context, such as a group or project, and invite a connection
  with its energetic essence. You might visualize the essence as
  a column of light or a ball of light. (If you are not visual, you
  may sense the essence without visualizing it.) Learn for yourself
  what happens when you connect with an essence for insights
  and support.

- Experiment with Conscious Co-Creation for a specific issue or challenge. Co-Creation means you bring your best knowledge, perspectives, and intentions to the table, and equally that you attune to the relevant essence, and welcome and act on its insights, perspectives, and recommendations.

- Often Conscious Co-Creation calls us to hold space for and to welcome what wants to emerge through our group or organization. This "holding space" requires us to be as open as possible to acting on opportunities and signals as they arise. ∧ Normally we are busy with what is already underway and how things have been done in the past. Holding space means being present to what is called for in this moment, and now in this moment, and now in this moment. It generally calls us to be comfortable with uncertainty. It invites us to say "Yes" to possibilities that feel intuitively right even when we do not know how they will work out. Such "Yesses" open space for emergence, which in turn supports innovation and transformation. ↺

  Paradoxically, when leaders are good at holding space (for co-creation), their organizations thrive, and yet those same leaders often have the feeling that they "are not doing anything." Value the act of holding space. It is like the goose that lays the golden eggs.

- It is helpful to keep your awareness as clear and open as possible. Imagine that you are a funnel and your project is the bottle. To be able to funnel energy and possibility from other levels into the project, you need to provide a clear pathway, free of blockages and obstructions. This means we need to deal with conflict and feelings of overload, inadequacy, and insecurity. ○ It does not have to take long, and it offers great benefits to your group – and of course to you!

  You might note what happens when individuals do not do the personal work of being clear and open: being in a group tends to amplify their personal issues, and these issues can bog the group down.

Intriguingly, stepping into a leadership position often brings latent personal issues to the surface. *If we want to create positive change on the outer, we must address the interior dimension.* A daily practice, such as Groundwork, meditation, yoga, a martial art, or journalling can help you "come home" to yourself and cultivate awareness that is clear and open.

- A key corollary of Conscious Co-Creation is to value *quality* more than *quantity*. Our mainstream society is addicted to growth and is caught in the myth that more is better. Rather than setting your course for growth or success defined monetarily, aim to be in harmony with life. Small acts done with pure love have more value than grand accomplishments based in ego or competition. Being true to yourself or to your organization's highest purpose, however small the act, has more value than great accomplishments on someone else's agenda. This is not to say that great accomplishments do not have value. Rather, the quality of intention and alignment matters more than the quantity of impact.

This means that to make the greatest contribution, we need to take time to know our life purpose and calling. In doing so, we will become familiar with the texture of when we are on track. Trust that quality of energy, and allow it to guide you. This is the best way to serve any group you are part of.

As you bring forth your authentic contributions, you will create opportunities for others to do the same, and help to bring your group and organization into greater harmony and alignment. As you pay attention to the quality of your essence, you will have the clarity and strength for "choiceless change." It will no longer be a struggle to bring forth your perspectives and offerings. You simply bring your best, and release.

Making your authentic offering is fulfilling in itself, and releases you from needing a particular outcome. Letting go of outcome, paradoxically, is what creates the most space for co-creation. You help create conditions for life to flow. Find the quality of being that is most aligned to you, and make it your guiding star.

Possible pitfalls

- Even people with years of experience acknowledge that some-times they are not clear enough to attune properly. This can be when they have a strong personal stake in the issue, or some personal baggage that keeps them stuck in the personality level. When this happens, the responsible thing to do is to withdraw from being part of the decision, analogous to abstaining where there is a conflict of interest.

- There can be a temptation to go straight to attunement, by-passing the gathering and sharing of information, perspectives, and insights. Conscious Co-Creation requires that people show up and bring the benefit of their knowledge, experience, and wisdom. Conscious Co-Creation is not about blindly following guidance alone, but bringing together the best of both worlds – the inner and the outer. ↻

- Another pitfall is imposing your guidance on others. This can happen when two or more people get different results in the same meditation. It can also happen when one person (or more) practices inner listening while others do not. In either case, it is important not to let the guidance you receive from an attunement have the final word. Guidance is often unanimous, and so simplifies many group deliberative processes. Where it is not unanimous, it may mean that the timing is not right, or that the question is not well framed, or that others do not accept this way of working.

At the personal level

What does it mean to apply Conscious Co-Creation at the personal level? There have been hints all through this chapter, and in the Groundwork chapter too. I hope you will try the many practical suggestions there.

At its core, Conscious Co-Creation calls us to love – both to recognize that love is what we are, in essence, and to express love in every facet of our lives. It invites us to embrace the paradox of being, at the same time, a separate self, and one with all that is: our unique very human self, and also at one/aligned with the interconnected and sacred intelligence of life.

To love is not something we do only once in a while. It is a way of being. It is a calling to be as awake and as conscious as we can be, and to intend to serve the highest/all of life.

When we show up this way – loving and dedicated to love – we are more likely to experience flow and synchronicity. These hallmarks are like sign posts, showing us we are on the right path.

Still, living co-creatively takes courage. It involves growing the "muscle" to trust again and again, both when things are going well and when they appear as though they are not. It involves being open to what life is saying, and to the nudges and prods of our intuition or signals, like the buzzing flies in Alan's story (see page 194). It involves taking leaps of faith, since life has a tendency to call us out of our comfort zone.

If you are lucky enough to have a sense of calling, or life purpose, then you already know the feeling texture of being in alignment with life. If the idea of life purpose does not resonate, that is fine. It is not required. What matters is an intention to be of service. If you are reading this book, you can trust that, fundamentally, you intend to benefit life.

The more you intend to serve all of life consciously and explicitly, the more life can co-create with you. Life is profoundly respectful. It will not impose its support upon us. We have to ask. We have to break the mindset of doing things on our own, and of being in control.

One more thing is asking to be said: the full phrase used at the Findhorn Foundation is Conscious Co-Creation with Nature. A simple way to nurture yourself and your ability to be in conscious co-creation with life is to connect with nature. This can be as simple as taking time to really see a houseplant, commune with a tree, or walk in a park. For stronger support, make a pilgrimage to a wild place such as an old growth forest, or immerse yourself in a river, lake, or ocean. When we do this with the intention of connecting to life, life can connect back more strongly. This nourishes us for the journey of being and becoming the love that we are in essence and of bringing that love to our world.

Links to other chapters

Conscious Co-Creation can boost the effectiveness of every other framework. Here are a few suggestions for cross-pollinating Conscious Co-Creation with other frameworks.

- Gain insight into the secondary process of your group (Process Work) by asking the overlighting essence what is seeking to unfold (Theory U).

- Connect with the overlighting energy of your initiative for insight into great ways to convene the "trinity of management" (Enterprise Facilitation).

- Cultivate your group's capacity for dialogue by attuning to the overlighting essence of the group at the beginning of a meeting/conversation (Generative Dialogue).

- Quicken the process of clarifying shared purpose by intending to align with the overlighting essence for your initiative (Chaordic Design).

See what happens when you try the suggestions for Conscious Co-Creation mentioned in this chapter. One of the greatest pieces of advice I received from an elder at the Findhorn Foundation was, "Experiment!" Like an artist, you can learn from others, but ultimately you have to find your own way.

For some starter suggestions of what to do Monday morning with this and the other nine tools, see the next chapter.

Questions

- Am I grounded, and connected to what is most alive in me?

- Are others in my context open to working co-creatively? If not, can I bring this way of working into the context through, for example, my internal state and how I frame issues?

- Am I bringing love to everything I do?

- Does our group have simple daily or weekly practices that keep us connected for working co-creatively?

- Are we open to, and grateful for, miracles (positive, unexpected, and not immediately explicable occurrences) large and small?

What To Do Monday Morning

A friend and colleague reviewed an early draft of this book. She loved the first seven frameworks but did not see herself as the right audience for the last three. Then she wrote, "If I think of your book as a cookbook, wanting to try 7 out of 10 recipes is, I figure, pretty darn good."

I agree!

Indeed, I am thrilled if all you take from this book is the value of working with frameworks, full stop. Bringing more awareness to our frames of reference is a powerful lever, and there are many other great frameworks out there.

Here are some possible next steps for using any of the frameworks in this book – or other frameworks you know and love.

Ways to integrate working with the frameworks

- Despite all the emphasis on working simultaneously with multiple frameworks, you should feel completely free to use just one. The depth of perspective we get from working with two or more is great. But seeing with one good eye is revolutionary compared to being "blind."

- Review the news of the day from the perspective of a particular framework, or a single news item from the perspective of multiple frameworks. I find Process Oriented Psychology and Appreciative Inquiry are great places to start.

- Keep a special journal where you note brief reflections at the end of each day inspired by one or more of the frameworks. Another option is regular reflective conversations with a learning buddy or buddies. Retrospectively considering meetings and group interactions from the frameworks' different points of view will quickly strengthen your "muscles" for being able to see group dynamics in the moment.

- Share the frameworks with a colleague, friend, or family member and support each other to engage with them. For example, Marika (see page 62) has shared her passion for the Generative Dialogue framework, and many of her colleagues have joined her in working with it consciously.

- Write one line that expresses what is most meaningful to you for each of the frameworks – either in general, or relating to a specific initiative. These "primary directives" can then be a customized checklist to help you quickly touch in on all the frameworks on a daily or weekly basis. See the One-liners sidebar for my current list.

- Take this book to your book club, or convene a study circle with others who agree to read one chapter a week for ten weeks, or two chapters a week for five weeks. Ask each other questions like, "What stands out? What does the framework help you see? How might you work with the framework in the coming week?"

Perhaps these ideas spark others of your own. If so, it would be great if you can share them through the *WeCanDoThisTools. com* website. The same goes for stories of your experiences, since nothing beats a good story for transferring knowledge and inspiring others.

One-liners

Framework	Primary Directive
Appreciative Inquiry	Focus on possibilities, not problems.
Chaordic Design	Be clear about purpose.
Generative Dialogue	Create conditions for conversations to be generative.
Adaptive Cycle	Be resilient over time.
Enterprise Facilitation	Facilitate access to the three key ingredients for success.
Theory U	Help to manifest the future seeking to emerge.
Process Oriented Psychology	Be aware of the moment by moment process in myself and my group.
Integral Theory	Do and be in ways that are Integral (all four quadrants).
Systemic Constellations	Attend to belonging, give and take, and social order.
Conscious Co-Creation	Co-create with Nature/Life.

Another way to work with the frameworks

Groups are as different as snowflakes, and they continue to change from meeting to meeting and from year to year. But all group processes can be looked at from the three perspectives of **before** the group gets together, **during** the meeting/group/system process, and **after** it is over.

As another way into working with the frameworks, and as a richer kind of checklist, see the following table for my current take on before, during, and after for each of the frameworks. You might put different one-liners in each box, or even a list of points. The idea is to find a simple way to review group situations from all ten perspectives.

Call to mind a current group situation you welcome insight into, and see what insights and inspirations you gain as you review the table on the next page.

Framework	Before	During	After
Appreciative Inquiry	• Frame topics/ invitations appreciatively. • Know and honour my strengths.	• Appreciate the group – focus on strengths and possibilities.	• Reflect on what was successful, and how to have more.
Chaordic Design	• Be crystal clear about purpose and principles: what are we really trying to do?	• Stay true to purpose and principles, and slow things down if need be.	• Review purpose and principles to see if still on track.
Generative Dialogue	• Create a high quality container for conversations; frame issues in potent ways.	• Suspend assumptions, let go of judgments, and listen deeply.	• Reflect on implications of the conversation for action going forward.
Adaptive Cycle	• Discern where we are in the adaptive cycle.	• Make changes, if called for, based on where we are in the adaptive cycle.	• Care for each other as we face change and implement tough decisions.
Enterprise Facilitation	• Put time into cultivating vibrant networks/ networkers.	• If relevant, convene the trinity of management.	• Strengthen the capacity of local people and systems to convene the trinity of management.

Framework	Before	During	After
Theory U	• Let go of the past structures and identities.	• Open to the future seeking to emerge.	• Keep refining rapid prototypes.
Process Oriented Psychology	• Look and listen for what is secondary in the group/ context and in myself.	• Act as an elder: support contributions from marginalized persons and perspectives.	• Reflect on any recurring themes for insights into the group's process.
Integral Theory	• Frame issues in ways that address all four quadrants.	• See the whole/part nature of everything, and watch for the twin dangers of collapsing and totalizing.	• Take action that is Integral (includes all four quadrants).
Systemic Constellations	• Honour those who have come before, and consider who rightfully belongs and needs to be part of the group process.	• Consider whether there are simple ways to make visible the hidden dynamics in the group, e.g. the four functions (see page 180).	• Balance Give and Take if things got out of whack either way during the group's process.
Conscious Co-Creation	• Connect on the inner to the essence of the group for insights and practical guidance.	• Attune to the essence of the group or initiative – e.g. for making decisions and gaining perspective.	• Give thanks for insights and assistance received on the inner.

I could go on with other ways into working with frameworks, but I sense this is enough. I do not want to bog things down with too many options. It stops being fun; and having fun with frameworks is key to a productive and long lasting relationship.

So, my almost final words ...

Have fun!

Coda: What is Possible

In 1992 I had an experience of group decision-making that has inspired me ever since. I include this story here as an invitation to keep exploring ways of seeing and being in groups that are win-win-win for individuals, communities, and the planet. We are just steps into whole new worlds of possibility!

At the same time, we are faced with the choice between fear and trust O more than ever before. Systems and structures are on the brink of collapse in every sector, and the longer we delay, the more issues cascade into other issues triggering ever more complex crises. ∞

The pressure is mounting. Almost everyone can feel it. Old ways of being have to fall away. We must shift from being lone wolves to co-creating with others, from accumulation to contribution, from control to dancing with the unknown.

I know in my bones that it is possible for groups at every level of society to work together in ways that seem miraculous by today's standards, the way StarTrek's wireless handheld communication devices, once so blue sky are now everywhere.

May the story below confirm that same knowing in you!

Co-creating breakthrough

The Findhorn Foundation staff group had gathered in the pale peach living room of Cullerne House, a grand and gracious mansion built from huge blocks of highland granite. Fifty plus of us sat in a ring of chairs interspersed with pillows on the floor.

Our purpose was to make the best possible decision about a highly contentious issue: should associate members of the wider community be represented on "Core Group" – the precious inner sanctum of the community?

The group was split. About half felt strongly that the Foundation had become inclusive enough, that associate members had not invested sufficient time or money the way members had, and that the meaning and privilege of membership should not be diluted further.

The other half believed that it was time to open up: some associates were more dedicated and committed than many members; not everyone had the financial and lifestyle freedom to be members (e.g. people with families); the Foundation was evolving and Core Group needed to reflect the new realities.

People felt strongly on both sides. We took time so that everyone who wanted to speak had a chance to be heard. Faces were often red with emotion.

After two hours it was clear that we had gone as far as we could at the personality level, and a respected elder staff member, trusted to be neutral, led us in a brief visualization.

We sat in silence together, with a very few words guiding us to have an inner knowing about what served the highest for all concerned.

After the meditation, the elder suggested we share the bottom line – simply saying "Yes" or "No" to including associate members on Core Group.

I will never forget the energy in the room as we spoke, one after the other, all around the circle.

"Yes."

"Yes."

"Yes ..."

With each "Yes" the atmosphere of the room got soupier, and in the end our decision was completely unanimous.

The unity was beautiful, profound, clean, unequivocal, and resonate. It was momentous and miraculous. We had stepped into a new way to be together, and everyone knew there was no going back.

Further Resources

Honourable Mentions – three additional frameworks

- **Systems Theory** – how systems (natural and human) evolve over time, including how short-term quick fixes tend to make things worse in the long run. See Peter Senge et al., *The Fifth Discipline Fieldbook: Strategies and Tools for Building a Learning Organization. London: Nicholas Brealey Publishing, 1994.*

- **Berkana Double Loop Model** – a theory of change for when existing institutions and structures are crumbling and emerging ones have yet to take up the slack. See http://berkana.org/about/our-theory-of-change/

- **Finite and Infinite Games** – contrasts human systems that are win-lose (finite) with those designed to keep the game going (infinite). See James P. Carse. *Finite and Infinite Games.* New York: Ballantine Books, 1987.

Groundwork

- Gibb, Jack. *Trust: A New Vision of Human Relationships for Business, Education, Family, and Personal Living.* Los Angeles, California: Guild of Tutors Press, 1978.

Appreciative Inquiry

- Cooperrider, David and Diana Whitney. *Appreciative Inquiry: Collaborating for Change.* San Francisco, California: Berrett-Koelher Publishers, Inc. 1999.

- Holman, Peggy, Tom Devane, and Steven Cady. *The Change Handbook: The Definitive Resource on Today's Best Methods for Engaging Whole Systems* (Second Edition). San Francisco, California: Berrett-Koelher Publishers, Inc., 2007.

- Appreciative Inquiry Commons. http://appreciativeinquiry.case.edu

Chaordic Design

- Hock, Dee. *The Birth of the Chaordic Age*. San Francisco, California: Berrett-Koehler Publishers, Inc., 1999.
- Chaordic Commons website. www.chaordic.org
- Hock, Dee. "The Art of Chaordic Leadership," *Leader to Leader Journal*, Volume 15, Winter 2000. Posted online in several places.
- Waldrop, M. Mitchell. "The Trillion-Dollar Vision of Dee Hock," *Fast Company*, October 31, 1996.

Generative Dialogue

- Isaacs, William. *Dialogue and the Art of Thinking Together*. New York, New York: Doubleday, 1999.
- Bohm, David. "Dialogue, a proposal," 1991. http://www.david-bohm.net/dialogue/dialogue_proposal.html
- Kahane, Adam. *Solving Tough Problems*. San Francisco, California: Berrett-Koehler Publishers, Inc., 2004.

Adaptive Cycle

- Gunderson, Lance and C. S. Holling. *Panarchy: Understanding Transformations in Human and Natural Systems*. Washington, DC: Island Press, 2001.
- Holling, C. S. 2004. "From complex regions to complex worlds." *Ecology and Society*, 9(1): 11. https://www.ecologyandsociety.org/vol9/iss1/art11/
- Holling, C.S. 2011. *Global Resilience Requires Novelty: A Speech by Buzz Holling*. https://aidontheedge.info/2011/10/25/global-resilience-requires-novelty-a-speech-by-buzz-holling/
- Westley, Frances, Brenda Zimmerman, and Michael Quinn Patton. *Getting to Maybe: How the World is Changed*. Toronto, Ontario: Random House Canada, 2006.
- Video: *Buzz Holling: father of resilience theory*. http://stockholmresilience.org/seminarandevents/seminarandeventvideos/buzzhollingfatheroftheresiliencetheory5.aeea46911a3127427980003713.html
- Resilience Alliance website. http://www.resalliance.org/

Enterprise Facilitation

- Sirolli, Ernesto. *Ripples from the Zambezi: Passion, Entrepreneurship, and the Rebirth of Local Economies*. Gabriola Island, British Columbia: New Society Publishers, 1999.

- Sirolli Institute website. www.sirolli.com
- Video: *Passion, Entrepreneurship and the Rebirth of Local Economies.* A TED Talk by Ernesto Sirolli telling the story of how he developed Enterprise Facilitation. http://www.youtube.com/watch?v=EBcidMBxXWM&feature=related

Theory U

- Scharmer, Otto. *Theory U: Leading from the Future as it Emerges.* San Francisco, California: Berrett-Koehler Publishers, Inc., 2009 and 2016.
- Scharmer, Otto and Katrin Kaufer. *Leading from the Emerging Future: From Ego-System to Eco-System Economies.* San Francisco, California: Berrett-Koehler Publishers, Inc., 2013.
- Senge, Peter, et al. *Presence: An Exploration of Profound Change in People, Organizations, and Society.* New York, New York: Doubleday, 2004.
- Presencing Institute website. http://www.presencing.com/
- Presencing Institute Community website. http://community.presencing.com/

Process Oriented Psychology

- Mindell, Arnold. *The Deep Democracy of Open Forums.* Charlottesville, Virginia: Hampton Roads Publishing Company, Inc., 2002.
- Mindell, Arnold. *The Leader as Martial Artist: An Introduction to Deep Democracy.* San Francisco, California: Harper, 1992.
- The Process Work Institute. www.processwork.org
- Deep Democracy Institute. www.deepdemocracyinstitute.org
- Burkhardt, Barbara. "The Missing Facilitator: An Exploration of the Concept of the Participant-Facilitator in Process Work," 2009. http://www.iapop.com/wp-content/uploads/2011/02/dissertations/burkhardt-missingfacilitator.pdf
- Stanford Siver. "Deep Democracy". http://stanfordsiver.net/deep-democracy/

Integral Theory

- Wilber, Ken. *A Theory of Everything: An Integral Vision for Business, Politics, Science, and Spirituality.* Boston, Massachusetts: Shambhala Publications, Inc., 2000.
- Wilber, Ken. *Sex, Ecology, Spirituality: The Spirit of Evolution.* Boston, Massachusetts: Shambhala Publications, Inc., 1995.

- Integral Institute website. in.integralinstitute.org
- Laloux, Frederic. *Reinventing Organizations: A Guide to Creating Organizations Inspired by the Next Stage of Human Consciousness.* Brussels, Belgium: Nelson Parker, 2014.

Systemic Constellations

- Hellinger, Bert, et. al. *Love's Hidden Symmetry: What Makes Love Work in Relationships.* Phoenix, Arizona: Zeig, Tucker and Co., 1998.
- Hellinger, Bert. *No Waves Without the Ocean: Experiences and Thoughts.* Heidelberg, Germany: Carl-Auer-Systeme-Verlag, 2006.
- Horn, Klaus, P. et al. *Invisible Dynamics; Systemic Constellations in Organisations and in Business.* Heidelberg, Germany: Carl-Auer-Systeme-Verlag, 2005.
- Stam, Jan Jacob. *Fields of Connection: The Practice of Organizational Constellations.* Avenhorn, The Netherlands: Systemic Books, 2016.
- Human Systems Institute, Resources page. https://www.human-systems-institute.com/resources/articles

Conscious Co-Creation

- McLean, Dorothy. *To Hear the Angels Sing.* Forres, Scotland: Findhorn Press, 1979.
- The Findhorn Community. *The Findhorn Garden: Pioneering a New Vision of Humanity and Nature in Cooperation.* Forres, Scotland: Findhorn Press, 1975.
- Hawken, Paul. *The Magic of Findhorn.* New York, New York: HarperCollins, 1975.
- Sutherland, Kate. *Make Light Work: 10 Tools for Inner Knowing.* Vancouver, British Columbia: Incite Press, 2010.

Other excellent resources

- Group Pattern Language Project, including the Group Works card deck. www.groupworksdeck.org.
- Kaner, Sam et al. *Facilitator's Guide to Participatory Decision-Making.* Gabriola Island, British Columbia: New Society Publishers, 1996.
- Block, Peter. *Community: The Structure of Belonging.* San Francisco, California: Berrett-Koehler Publishers, Inc., 2008.

Acknowledgements

Many wonderful people have been integral to this journey. I am particularly grateful for:

- The brilliant and pioneering work of the creators of the ten frameworks – David Cooperrider, Dee Hock, C.S. Holling, Arnold Mindell, Otto Scharmer, Ernesto Sirolli, Ken Wilber, Bert Hellinger, and founders of the Findhorn Foundation, Peter and Eileen Caddy and Dorothy McLean – along with the thousands who have built on and developed each of these bodies of work. Also Jack Gibb for his Trust Theory, a key foundation for the Groundwork chapter.

- The generosity of the storytellers who shared their experiences of working with specific frameworks: Brita Adkinson, Lane Ayre, Doug Cohen & Jonathan Cloud, Tatiana Glad, Glen Griggs, Marilyn Hamilton, Maureen Jack-LaCroix, Catherine Matthias, Jane Peterson, Marika Sandrelli, Otto Scharmer, and Alan Watson.

- Evan Renaerts, my friend and husband, for believing in me, for carrying more of the load as I was writing, and for brilliant solutions to thorny issues; and to my daughter Emma for cups of tea, brilliant editing, and loving support.

- Members of the circle review process who commented on draft chapters of *Make Light Work in Groups* (the earlier version of this book), through a series of ten weekly conference calls: Sabine Amend, Lauren Bacon, Sue Biely, Doug Cohen, Jodi Lasseter, Peggy Schultz, John Stoddart, Jane Sutherland, and Anne Thompson.

- Other early readers of specific chapters or the whole of *Make Light Work in Groups* whose comments helped bring greater depth and clarity: Suzanne Barois, Barbara Burkhardt, Karen Clarke, Jeanie Cockell, Diana Ellis, Olivia Fermi, Darlene Gage, Anne Kaye, Darcy Riddell, Stanford Siver, Lena Soots, and Marilyn Waller. Also Saskia Wolsak for brilliant developmental editing and her deep insight into group dynamics.

- Barbara Joughin and Joanne Kembel for insightful editing, scouring the text, and loving attention to detail. Having the same team for all three of my books has been such a gift!

- Lauren Bacon for her insightful comments on the roughest draft of *Make Light Work in Groups,* and for her close companionship in the journey of revising, producing, and promoting that book.

- Kaz Brecher for nudging me to create this new version of the book, and others in the THNK community for love, support, consultations, feedback, and brilliant advice and services – with special mention to Sarah Dickinson and Jess Fraser.

- Jane Peterson for generously sharing her deep knowledge, experience, and insight relating to Systemic Constellations, and for helping me draft a better introduction to this framework than I ever could have done on my own.

- The 200+ people who backed the Indiegogo campaign that funded the production costs for this new version. Having this backing has been a constant and wonderful source of moral support, as well as helpful financing for such new features as the illustrations.

- Michael Mann for distilling complex ideas into powerful illustrations, and for being so fun to work with.

- Hilary Henegar for showing up out of the blue, in perfect timing, to help me lay the groundwork for growing a movement to revolutionize how we work together.

- Vanessa LeBourdais for wise counsel, quick turnaround feedback, loving support, and companionship on the journey of living one's full potential as a change maker.

- Jane Sutherland, my mother and associate, for introducing me to Trust Theory, for the quality of the space she holds for brainstorming and problem solving, and for wise and helpful comments on the different chapters.

- Robert Sutherland, my father, for nurturing a life-long love of big picture ways of seeing.

About the Author

Kate Sutherland has a passion for supporting individuals and groups to become more aligned with their core purpose, and thus more innovative and impactful. She is increasingly focused on helping leaders and change agents create non-linear change through inner work (i.e. intention, perception, intuition, and consciousness). Knowing the latent capacity in groups for collective intelligence, co-creation, and flow, she is dedicated to fostering the movement to unfold the collective dimensions of human potential.

A social entrepreneur and organizational development consultant, Kate has worked on issues as diverse as the environment, food, social cooperatives, the sharing economy, recovery, early child development, and community inclusion. Often her work involves bridging mindsets, stakeholders, sectors, and silos, while also creating dynamic, high trust environments that support groups to be self-organizing, generative, and fun.

Kate is founding faculty and executive coach with THNK School of Creative Leadership (Vancouver), a global executive leadership program founded in Amsterdam. In 2016 she co-designed a Social Innovation Certificate program for Simon Fraser University where she continues as co-faculty and executive coach.

We Can Do This! is Kate's third book, after *Make Light Work: 10 Tools for Inner Knowing* (2009), and the earlier version of this book, *Make Light Work in Groups: 10 Tools to Transform Meetings, Companies, and Communities* (2012).

Kate is married and has one daughter. She loves hiking, cycling, swimming, and resting in the stillness that is the source of everything. She lives with her family in Vancouver's Little Mountain area.